Helping Children Choose:

Resources, Strategies, and Activities for Teachers of Young Children

Good Year® Education Series
Theodore W. Hipple, Editor

More GOOD YEAR BOOKS® in Science, Math, and Social Studies

For information about these or any Good Year Books®, please write to

Good Year Books
Scott, Foresman and Company
1900 East Lake Avenue
Glenview, Illinois 60025

George M. Schuncke
UNIVERSITY OF FLORIDA
Suzanne Lowell Krogh
UNIVERSITY OF FLORIDA

Helping Children Choose:

Resources, Strategies, and Activities for Teachers of Young Children

Scott, Foresman and Company
Glenview, Illinois   Dallas, Texas   Oakland, New Jersey
Palo Alto, California   Tucker, Georgia   London

For Matthew, Mark, and Peter

23456 EBI 88 87 86

ISBN: 0-673-16622-8

Contents

Decision Stories

The Importance of Decision Making

The Development of Moral Skills

We recently accepted an invitation to dinner at the home of some acquaintances we see occasionally. A few days later, a dear friend whose company we always thoroughly enjoy asked us to dinner on the same night. We would have much preferred visiting this closer friend, but we had to say no, without seriously considering whether we would accept this invitation and back out of the first one. We declined because of our conviction that we must do all we can to honor commitments, and we had made a commitment when we accepted the first invitation, after all.

Our decision was practically automatic and in that respect unthinking, but it was not unthinking in the sense of being morally or ethically ungrounded. A personal set of values helped us decide what to do, as it does all responsible adults who face social choices. Whether we decide between conflicting dinner invitations or more important alternatives—those involved in elections, for instance—we weigh the consequences of the

1

courses of action available to us in terms of our personal beliefs about what is good and right. Then we act in accordance with these beliefs. In short, consciously or not, we try to base social action on logically coherent choice.

Learning to choose what to do when there are important issues involved requires the ability to make conscious rational decisions, the ability to empathize, and the ability to reflect on experiences so as to be able to generalize from them. These decision, empathy, and reflection skills do not emerge full-blown when one enters adulthood but are the result of gradual development that begins in childhood. This development is not automatic in speed or direction. Left to their own devices, children are inclined to choose on the basis of immediacy—what seems best for the present moment. They have little concept of the future implications of any choice because they are not fully aware that what is happening now can affect their lives later. In addition, they often do not realize that there might be alternative ways of dealing with a problem. Because they cannot envision alternative courses of action, they cannot conceive of alternative consequences. In fact, their orientation to the here and now may prevent their imagining even one future consequence of some present course of action.

Teaching Decision Making

Adults, including teachers, can help children develop the skills of reasoning, empathizing, and valuing. We discuss theories about these skills in chapter six; here we briefly look at them from a practical point of view, indicating what they are and how they can be developed in the classroom.

Social Reasoning

Social reasoning in decision making involves the systematic steps that we take from the moment of realization that we need to decide something to the point of decision itself. Children learn these steps through reflection on repeated experience with making decisions, and children can reflect more fruitfully than otherwise with a teacher's help.

Social reasoning in decision making also involves the attitudes and ideas we bring to bear on a problem. William Damon (1977) has found that, at different points in their lives, children tend to bring to a dilemma different ideas about the world and their place in it, according to recognizable stages. And as children progress to higher stages of social reasoning, their thinking becomes more thorough, complex, and useful to them.

Damon has found that children move to higher stages of social reasoning when they are allowed to interact with each other in considering social problems that are real to them—those they face in their own experience (as opposed to the problems adults think important).

In order to understand their thinking about social issues, Damon has interviewed children extensively, using open-ended stories like those in chapter four of this book. One of the social issues Damon has explored is that of fairness in sharing, or, as he calls it, positive justice. In one of his stories, a group of children who have made paintings to sell at a school fair face the dilemma of how to divide the profits. We have used this same story in our own research and can confirm some of Damon's observations. Children of about five years, for example, think that the profits should be split evenly, no matter how hard anybody worked. First and second graders, on the other hand, begin to look at the merit of each participant's contribution to the effort that yielded the profit: someone who painted more pictures should get more of the money.

Damon was concerned with developmental theory; we were interested in classroom teaching. Happily, we found that if we presented open-ended stories to children and then led them in structured classroom discussion or in role play, the students measurably progressed in their reasoning. First graders, for example, who were still arguing, a la kindergartners, that everyone should get the same share of profits from the sale of the paintings in Damon's story began to weigh merit of contribution when we worked with them according to the program outlined in this book.

Empathizing

Empathizing in decision making involves imagining how others feel if we act in certain ways. As with social reasoning, this ability to take the perspective of others is developmental in nature. Robert Selman (1976) observed that young children cannot see a social situation from any point of view but their own. Gradually, they learn to perceive situations from the standpoints of others; finally, they learn to look objectively at such situations from a third-person point of view. Selman calls this empathizing *social perspective taking*, and he researched its stages, again, by presenting children open-ended stories. In one, a young boy's dog has disappeared, and the boy has announced that he never wants to own another dog, not ever. Two of his friends have an opportunity to buy him a puppy for his birthday, and they ask themselves, "How will he really feel?" Very young children, Selman found, answered this question without ambivalence. They were sure that a new, cute puppy would make the unhappy boy very happy and that he would abandon his earlier attitude. Older children, however, were not as sure. They were better able to put themselves in the boy's shoes; they could empathize with his ambivalent feelings.

Selman has indicated that teachers can help children grow through the stages of social perspective taking, as our research with open-ended stories used with structured discussion and role play confirms. Children who were sure buying the puppy was a good idea, for example, began to understand that the issue was more complex.

Valuing

Although decision making is an intellectual activity, it ultimately requires that all the options we imagine, and their consequences, be evaluated against a set of fundamental beliefs that we hold. We are not born with this set of values, nor does one automatically emerge. Again, adults have an influence; indeed, adults at home and in religious centers are deeply involved in shaping the development of children's values. Teachers, too, are influential, whether they want to be or not. Values permeate any curriculum and any classroom. They underlie stereotypes in textbooks, are reflected even in seating arrangements and names of reading groups, become explicit in classroom rules against cheating on tests, resonate in the social issues that emerge from time to time in the classroom. Surely teachers could ignore the value-laden aspects of teaching only by ignoring the facial expressions and body language of the children, their explicit and implied verbal messages, and their classroom social life. Success in this effort would be no small accomplishment.

We believe that, because values are integral to classroom life, teachers must address them. In addition, because values and the process of valuing develop over time, we also believe that a consideration of them must begin at the earliest grades and continue through the school years. Now, the two current major classroom approaches to addressing values were developed generally for children in the middle or higher grades. These two approaches are values clarification, and the encouragement of moral development as Lawrence Kohlberg defines it. Values clarification, as described by Raths, Harmin, and Simon (1966), focuses on choosing—freely, from alternatives, after thorough consideration of consequences; prizing—esteeming the choice, and being willing to affirm it publicly; and acting—repeatedly doing something on the basis of the choice. Teachers using values clarification encourage students to improve these component skills through a variety of written and verbal strategies.

The second classroom approach is a curricular application of Lawrence Kohlberg's cognitive-developmental theory of moralization. Kohlberg says children develop from moral egocentrism to a self-transcending respect for the structure of law and society, and then, if they are among the morally gifted few, to a true concern for universal principles of justice. One grows morally, according to this school of thought, because of exposure to higher stages of moral reasoning than one's own; one is naturally attracted to that reasoning and abandons one's own in its favor. The key to this exposure is, of course, interaction with others.

School programs that apply Kohlberg's theory use open-ended stories called moral dilemmas, which the students discuss among themselves. Research has shown that children in the middle and higher grades do indeed advance in skill in moral reasoning by means of these discussions.

Although most of the materials used with these approaches have been developed for older students, both values clarification and Kohlberg's scheme are useful for teachers of early grades. Our own program owes much to both of them. We have essentially made concrete the rather abstract techniques of these two approaches shown to be successful with older students, in order that young children may grasp them.

An Approach for Young Children

Teaching social decision making to young children requires that we structure activities that develop reasoning, perspective-taking, and valuing skills, and that these activities be appropriate to young children's levels of cognitive development. We know, for example, that children in their early years and throughout grade school learn best by manipulating concrete materials and by focusing on issues that are close to them in space and time. This implies that decision-making experiences in the elementary school are more instructive if they include hands-on activities, if the topics have personal significance to the children, and if the teacher involves every child actively in every learning event. If the activities are abstract or remote, or require capabilities that the children do not possess, the children do not learn much.

We wrote this book to help you address social decision making with children in kindergarten through at least third grade. We present open-ended stories we have found in our research to be effective with children as young as kindergartners. The children themselves determined the content of these stories. Over a period of several months, we interviewed children in all the elementary grades about what social values were most important to them. The results of this study are the foundation of the open-ended stories we have provided for your use. We call them decision stories. We discuss how we developed them so that you can prepare your own, if you wish.

We also share strategies for helping children grow in social decision making. We have found these strategies help children grow significantly in reasoning, perspective-taking, and valuing capabilities.

In the first chapter, we give you an overview of the techniques and materials we recommend. Chapters two and three expand on the techniques. Chapter four contains materials, including visual aids that you may reproduce. Chapter five tells you how to develop your own materials. Chapter six discusses the work of educators and theorists of moral development who have influenced our classroom research and is especially recommended if you plan to develop your own materials. Finally, we provide an annotated bibilography that you will find useful if you wish to explore further the theoretical underpinnings of this curriculum.

A 1-2-3 Approach to Teaching

How To Use Decision Stories

Tom sees his best friend, Eric, cheating on a spelling test. Should he tell the teacher or not?

Judy has a feeling that her good friend Allison has taken money from her friend Jennifer's purse. What should she do?

Everybody's trading lunches, but Mark's mother told him to eat everything she packed. He wants to be like all the other kids. He wonders if just this once she wouldn't mind . . .

Dilemmas like these are common to children's lives. They present conflicts between values that children hold as roughly equal in importance. Tom, for example, believes that friendship is valuable, but he also thinks that people should be honest when they take tests. He must decide upon which belief he will act.

To help children like Tom, Judy, and Mark resolve such conflicts in their own lives, we have developed a teaching resource we call the decision story. All the materials and strategies we present in this book revolve around it. In this chapter, we say what it is and why we developed it. Then we discuss two ways to teach with decision stories: using role play, and leading structured discussion.

Decision Stories

What Are Decision Stories?

A *decision story* is an open-ended story the completion of which requires resolution of a conflict.

By open-ended story, we mean one that has no specified resolution but can be completed in a variety of ways. There is no set, correct ending to an open-ended story; any alternative that a child might suggest is appropriate for consideration.

By conflict in an open-ended story, we mean a dilemma that the main character faces because of competing claims. The children with whom we have worked seem to value seven social goods above all others: telling the truth, obeying people in authority, obeying rules, respecting other people's property, sharing, keeping promises, and honoring friendship. A conflict occurs when a child cannot act in accord with one of these values except at the expense of another.

To give you a better idea of how these values can conflict for children, and to illustrate the structure of an open-ended story, we here present "Adrian's Sunday," one of the decision stories in chapter four. It is primarily intended for use with middle and upper elementary children.

It was another dull Sunday afternoon. Adrian was really bored. This Sunday was worse than others because Lynn, Adrian's best friend, was at her grandmother's house for the weekend. At least when Lynn was here, they could find something to do. Today, however, just dragged and dragged. As she was trying for what felt like the hundredth time to think of something to do, the phone rang.

"Hi, Adrian, this is Stacy. What are you doing?"

"Nothing."

"Well, why don't you come over to my house? My parents are going to visit some people, and I don't want to go with them. They said I could stay home if one of my friends came over and kept me company. Do you want to come? We can play records on the stereo."

Adrian was surprised. She hadn't been particularly friendly with Stacy. In fact, she and Lynn seldom said anything more than hi to her. Stacy was okay, but Adrian and Lynn had a good time just hanging around with each other.

Adrian paused a moment. "Well, okay," she said. There really wasn't anything else to do anyway.

"Good. I'm so glad I don't have to go with them. It's so boring. Here, tell my mother that you'll come. She said I couldn't stay home alone."

After Adrian told Stacy's mother that she would come over, Adrian gathered some records to take with her.

Just as she started to leave, the phone rang again.

"Adrian," an excited voice on the phone said, "it's Lynn. We came home early. You've got to come right over and see the things my grandmother gave me."

"What did you get?" Adrian asked.

"Oh, lots of really neat things. When are you coming?"

"Well," Adrian said . . .

The open-endedness of the story is obvious; Adrian can do a number of things. She can, of course, cancel the afternoon with Stacy, or tell Lynn that she cannot come. She might also lie to Stacy, or she could lie to Lynn. She might ask Stacy if she could bring Lynn along. You may have thought of other possibilities. The story does not lead to one or two specific solutions, but is open to many and various endings, any of which might be suggested by children in real life. We have found, incidentally, that children come up independently with almost any answer a teacher could have suggested—and some surprise endings as well.

The values that conflict in Adrian's story are those of remaining true to a friendship (with Lynn) and keeping a promise (to Stacy, a less close friend). We developed this story because the elementary children we interviewed indicated that friendship and keeping promises were both very important to them.

You might note, too, that the issue in this story is the one we describe in the Introduction, a problem we ourselves faced. Indeed, children who learn to sort out ethical issues consciously are learning to navigate the waters that responsible adults must sail in everyday life.

Why Use Decision Stories?

Children in kindergarten and the elementary grades learn best in a concrete manner. Topics, concepts, and materials must be close to them in time and space. Children learning to choose must see the relationship to their own lives of the decisions to be made. Only then can they become more skillful in a generalized way at making decisions. Decision stories meet this criterion of concreteness. We have tested them with children and found that students attend them well and learn from them. In addition, we encourage you to use our model to create decision stories of your own that are particularly relevant to your students; see chapter five.

The 1-2-3 Approach

Anyone connected with education has probably heard, somewhere along the way, the adage that dictates three steps in teaching: Tell them what you're going to teach them, teach them, and then tell them what you taught them. After the students have been told and then told and then told, it is assumed they have learned something.

We disagree with this assumption in one respect: telling alone will not necessarily do the trick, especially with very young children. They learn by doing: interacting, observing, handling, acting in various ways. In fact, they will hardly sit still to be told anything three times.

We agree, however, that three teaching steps are warranted. We find that good teachers almost always warm up a class in some way before getting to the heart of the matter, and also devote time to some sort of closure afterward. Our 1-2-3 approach, for use with decision stories, reflects this observation.

What Is the 1-2-3 Approach?

The 1-2-3 approach involves a warm-up, an action period, and a debriefing.

The *warm-up* gets the students ready to learn. One of its functions is to kindle students' interest in the problem at hand and motivate them to explore it. They hear the decision story and become thoroughly acquainted with the various facets of the problem. Finally, the warm-up is a time of practical preparation: what will be done in the action period, and how it will be done, are decided, and specific tasks are allocated.

The *action period* demands the children's active (but not necessarily physical) involvement. We suggest two alternatives for the action period, role play and structured discussion.

In *role play*, children are either players or observers. The players act out suggested solutions to the problem presented in the open-ended story; the observers involve themselves intellectually and emotionally.

In *structured discussion*, children suggest alternative endings to the decision story and spell out the consequences of each. The suggestions are mapped out on a chart. The mode of representation depends on the age of the children in the class: with younger children, simple pictures or symbols are used; for those able to read, the suggestions can be written on the chart.

The *debriefing* is a time for examining and evaluating what occurred in the action period. The teacher and students together reflect on what the children did, how they did it, and how appropriate the activity was. Usually, the class comes to conclusions about the issue at hand during the debriefing.

The teacher leads the debriefing, directing the children toward a rational choice. In the action period, the children had the opportunity to explore alternate solutions to the problem presented by the decision story and to become aware of the consequences attendant on each of them. Now they can decide which is perhaps the most appropriate resolution. The teacher

2

Putting Oneself in Another's Shoes

Role Play and How To Do It

"Hey, that's a new game! Can I see it?"

If a child said this to you, you probably wouldn't hold the game at a distance while the child simply looked at it. You know the child means, "May I touch it; turn it over; look at it closely; sniff it, maybe; try out its mechanical possibilities?" For a young child, especially, there is more to seeing then using the eyes.

For young children, there is also more to discussing a problem than talking about it. When they can act it out, explore its solutions physically, turn it over in their minds, and finally talk about it, too, then young children really discuss. That is why we recommend role play as the primary technique to use with the discussion of decision stories with young children. When children approach the middle elementary years, more traditional, formal discussion can begin to play a larger part in successful consideration of problems. Yet, even kindergartners should be introduced

15

to structured discussion, and older children still benefit from role play. For this reason, we urge you to use both strategies with your children, whatever their grade level. We present this chapter on role play and the following chapter on structured discussion to help you do so. Which technique you emphasize depends on the ages of the children you teach, on the demands of each situation, and on what works best for your students and for you.

As we talk about role play and structured discussion, we give specific suggestions for the different uses of each technique with younger and older children. It is up to you to decide which level of maturity your students have reached. If your third graders, for instance, are cognitively relatively mature and have participated in role play and classroom discussion for the last couple of years, they probably fit our definition of older children. On the other hand, if their experiences have been more structured and have involved little or no group interaction, they may respond best to approaches we say are for younger children. By the same token, structured discussion is sometimes appropriate for children as young as kindergartners. Read the descriptions of the activities, try them with your children, and observe closely. No one will be a better judge of what works best than you.

As we indicate in chapter one, both role play and structured discussion involve the 1-2-3 approach to using decision stories: warm-up, action period, and debriefing. In this chapter, we say how these steps apply to role play. Our discussion is based to some extent on the work of Fannie and George Shaftel, whose book *Role Playing in the Curriculum* provides an in-depth view of the process and techniques of role play, and is a classic in the field (see "Further Reading"). We make our general points about the 1-2-3 approach here by describing how you would apply it to a specific decision story in chapter four. This story, "The Car Crash," is appropriate for either kindergartners or first graders. It presents a conflict between the values of keeping a promise and telling the truth, primarily; it also raises issues involving respect for property, authority, and friendship.

Robert was playing in the block corner, building a small house, all by himself. And he was watching Mitchell and Brian build a garage with some bigger blocks.

Robert heard Mitchell say, "I'm tired of building this garage. I'm going to the easel and paint."

"Okay," said Brian, "but will you leave your red car here? I want to play with it."

"Sure," Mitchell answered, "but take good care of it, because I just got it for my birthday." Then Mitchell went to the easel.

Robert kept on building his small house, and he kept on watching Brian build the garage. He saw Brian start to zoom the red racing car around and over the garage. Suddenly the car crashed into a block wall, and a car door fell off.

"Uh-oh," Robert said, "Mitchell's going to be mad at you."

Brian looked very worried. "Don't tell on me," he begged. "I didn't *mean* to break it!"

Robert thought for a moment. Brian was his good friend, and he didn't want him to get in trouble. "Okay," he said, "I won't tell."

Brian took the red racing car and put it in Mitchell's cubby. He tried to make the door look as though it was still on.

After a while, the teacher said it was time to clean up.

"Where's my racing car?" Mitchell asked Brian.

"I put it in your cubby," Brian answered.

Mitchell went to his cubby and took the car out. The door fell to the floor with a clatter.

"Oh, no!" Mitchell cried. "What did you do to my car, Brian?"

"Nothing," said Brian. "I didn't break it."

Mitchell took his red car to the teacher. "Somebody broke my car," he said.

The teacher gathered all the children around her. "Who broke Mitchell's car?" she asked.

"I didn't," everybody said—even Brian.

Mitchell looked at Brian. "I'll bet you did it!" he yelled.

"I did not!" Brian yelled back.

Robert looked at them both. Then he looked at the teacher. She seemed very angry. First he remembered that he'd promised his friend Brian not to tell. He knew that Brian hadn't broken the car on purpose.

Then the teacher said, "If somebody knows what really happened, please say so. It's very important to tell the truth."

"Oh, dear," thought Robert, "what should I do now?"

The Warm-up

As the leader of role play, you have a variety of tasks to accomplish in the warm-up. You want to get the children interested in the issue the story raises and motivated to hear the open-ended story itself. You must present the story; then you must facilitate the suggestion of resolutions to it. Finally, you have to choose children to act out these possible solutions, and you must prepare the rest of the children to watch the action carefully. Each of these tasks takes little time, but each is very important.

Preparation for Listening

We have found several strategies that do a good job of preparing children to hear the decision story. They all encourage the children to pay attention to people's feelings, specifically, the feelings that emerge in the kind of situation to be explored in the role play.

Using Concrete Objects

Because young children are especially attracted to objects they can see, hold, touch, and smell, you can gain their attention by presenting a tangible object that is in some way related to the story they will hear. First, introduce the object to the children, and make certain they know what it is. Next, ask their impressions, and possibly feelings, about the object. Then direct the discussion toward the subject of feelings about the object in situations like the one that will emerge in the story.

The use of a concrete object is especially appropriate in a warm-up for "The Car Crash" because the story revolves around a tangible (Mitchell's new toy car), and because the story is aimed at very young children. You might begin the warm-up by showing the children a small toy car and asking them if they know what it is. Just about everyone will be familiar with toys like it, and some children, no doubt, will discuss similar toys they have had. You might then say, "This is a nice car, isn't it? How would you feel if it were yours and somebody broke it?" After listening to their feelings about having a toy broken, you might then ask, "Suppose you were the person who broke it, but you didn't do it on purpose. How would you feel?" Learning to step outside a situation and see it from other viewpoints is essential in learning to make value judgments, but it is not easy for young children to do. They may be a bit startled at first when you ask them to look at different sides to the story. However, with your help they can begin to do this. Finally, introduce the story, by saying, for instance, "I want to tell you a story about some boys who had a problem with a toy's being broken. I want you to listen carefully and think about what they could do about this problem."

Using Children's Own Experiences

Just as children are attracted to concrete objects, they also enjoy telling others about their own experiences and comparing them with those of their peers. You can interest the children in the issue at hand by asking them to talk about incidents in their lives that parallel incidents in the decision story.

Begin with a question that gets the children thinking about a situation like the story's. Then ask the children how they have felt in this sort of situation. Ask next how others involved in the situation might have felt. Finally, introduce the story, telling the children that they are going to hear about a problem involved in just such a situation. Ask them to try to think up solutions to this problem.

With "The Car Crash," you might begin by asking the children, "How many of you have had a new toy?" and then, "Who would like to tell us about it?" Once the children have responded briefly to these questions, ask about emotions, saying something like, "How would you feel if your new toy broke?" Then, to get the children to look at the situation from another viewpoint, you might say, "Suppose you broke someone else's new toy and didn't do it on purpose. How would you feel then?" After hearing their responses, invite them to listen to the story by saying, "Let's listen to a story about a problem some boys had. It's very much like this problem we've been talking about. Let's see if we can figure out what they can do."

Using the Teacher's Own Experiences

Although not generally as potent a strategy as using concrete objects or the children's own experiences, telling about things that have happened to you, the teacher, can work well in a warm-up. Your students are interested in your experiences. They want to know what you are like outside the classroom, and they are happy to learn that you encountered some of the same problems growing up that they run into now.

First, ask a "Have you ever . . . ?" question related to the problem the children will hear about in the decision story. (Have them answer just yes or no; you want to get their attention, not engage them in discussion.) Then talk about a similar problem you faced during childhood. Emphasize the problematic nature of the situation rather than its specific resolution; otherwise, you may unwittingly preempt the children's later choice. Talk about your feelings in the situation, and be sure to say how others might have felt, too. Then ask the children to listen to a story about a similar situation.

One of us had an experience as a child that could be recounted as follows to introduce "The Car Crash." "One Christmas, when I was eight years old, my five-year-old brother got a toy bow and arrow set as a gift on Christmas morning. I wanted to play with it, too, but he wouldn't let me, all day. After dinner, he finally let me try it out, as long as he could keep an eye on me the whole time. Unfortunately, neither of us realized that, because I was a lot bigger and stronger than my brother, the bow was too small and fragile for me. On my third pull, the bow cracked in half. My younger brother started to cry because his present was ruined and I felt awful because I knew how much my brother had wanted that present, and also because I knew our parents might be angry when they found out what had happened."

To use this account in a warm-up for "The Car Crash," one would first ask, "How many of you ever broke a toy that belonged to someone else?" and then, after the children have raised their hands, "How many of you have ever had a toy that was broken by someone else?" The anecdote about the broken bow would then be told. Finally, the teacher would ask the children to listen to a story about a similar problem.

Discussing the Issues Themselves

This strategy, discussing in advance the issues the story raises, is for children who are quite experienced with decision stories. If your class is still most attracted to warm-ups that begin with concrete objects, or if it is just beginning to think about issues involving values, then this strategy will not work well.

Discussing the issues themselves in the warm-up involves moving the discussion of general moral questions from its usual place in the debriefing to an earlier slot in the schedule. This requires the children to begin the role-play experience with more or less philosophical thought. It can work, but only, as we say, if the children are experienced. It is also advisable for them to have discussed the same issues in previous sessions.

For example, the class might recently have role-played possible solutions to a conflict between keeping a promise and telling the truth. This time, you might begin a session that involves one or the other of these issues with a question like "Why do people say you should keep a promise?" or "Is it always a good idea to keep a promise? When might it not be a good idea?" If you want to focus on telling the truth, you might ask, "Is it always important to tell the truth?" After the questions have been discussed and the students are interested, introduce the story itself, saying something like, "Let me tell you a story in which some boys have a problem that involves just these questions."

There may be times when you want to focus on a particular issue or when you see that the class has a need for such a focus, and this type of warm-up will provide the continuity you need.

Presentation of the Story

Telling an open-ended story involves special considerations. First, choose the story carefully. The issue that the story raises should represent a real conflict between at least two values that the children hold in high esteem. All the decision stories in chapter four present such conflicts—for children in the grades indicated in the upper left-hand corner above each story. If you develop your own story, on the other hand, consult chapter five, "Making Your Own," to see which values conflict for children at your students' grade level and which do not.

In addition to presenting a real conflict in values, the story you choose should be one that is vivid but not threatening to the children. The plot should be close to their experience, but not close to any particularly intense problem they are actually facing. For example, if there is a problem with the theft of money in your classroom, you might use a story that concerns the stealing of food or toys in a nonschool setting.

The particulars of the story itself should be relevant, too. In "The Car Crash," all the characters are boys. You might want to make them all girls, or mix sexes. You might want to change the toy to something you know is especially attractive to your students. Or you might change some of the language in the story, if you know your students would phrase things differently. Do not hesitate to change the stories in this book to suit your situation.

Presenting a decision story is more challenging than presenting an ordinary story, and you must prepare. You are going to tell the story instead of reading it, if possible, especially if your students are very young. This permits more or less continuous eye contact, which helps keep the children's attention and lets you verify that they understand what you are saying. So read the story to yourself several times beforehand to acquaint yourself thoroughly with its plot. Do not try to memorize it; just be certain of its basic elements. At least the first few times, you may also want to practice your actual storytelling, perhaps in front of a mirror.

With older children, too, telling the story is usually preferable to reading it, but it is not always necessary. You can get away with less preparation than with younger children, to be blunt—but your enthusiasm is just as necessary.

As you tell the story to the children, you must sound as morally neutral as possible; be careful to keep your opinions to yourself. Children, even older ones, consider their teacher the voice of authority, and they will mimic your attitudes, if you are not careful, without learning to make choices themselves. This is not to suggest that you tell the stories in a monotone, but your intonations and facial expressions should not give away your judgment about the action or characters.

Eliciting Alternative Solutions and Choosing Those To Be Acted Out

When you say the last words of the story, if you simply look expectant, the children may automatically begin to offer resolutions. Or you might end a story such as "The Car Crash" by saying, "Well, what *will* Robert do?" Ask what a character will do rather than what he or she should do, because a "should" question often elicits responses designed to be acceptable to authority, as opposed to what the children actually think ought to happen, given their own beliefs and experiences. Whatever you choose to say or do, convey to the students that any idea is acceptable, and you are ready to receive them all. Your job is to elicit as many endings as the children can possibly invent, without passing judgment in any public way.

As you ask children to suggest solutions to the decision story's problem, one of four things is likely to happen. Some of these four things can be disconcerting to a teacher, but, with special handling, all can help the students learn.

Only One Solution

If the class suggests only one solution, it is possible that the story is not appropriate at this time, that the children may all be thinking on the same track just now, or that they simply have not had enough experience yet to think further. In any event, let the children act the solution out, and work on the assumption that the enactment itself may generate ideas about other ways of handling the problem. In many cases, this is exactly what happens. If it does not, you carry the role play to its conclusion—debriefing the enactment, using techniques we discuss below; choose another problem to be role-played; or end the session.

No Solutions

If there are no suggestions at all, perhaps the children, although they understand the problem, cannot think immediately of any solutions to it. One way to help younger children begin imagining solutions is to have them enact the entire decision story; this acting out may direct their thinking to potential solutions to the problem. If possible, children should take the roles of all the characters. At times, however, you may find it necessary to take a role yourself, to get things going. In this role, which should be that of one of the minor characters, you must not suggest a course of action; rather, ask the major character leading questions that move him or her to decide a direction.

If older children have no suggestions, focus on characters instead of solutions. That is, ask the children what the characters are like, how they feel, what they are thinking, and how they therefore might act. When the children better understand the characters, they can better think as the characters would and suggest solutions the characters themselves might adopt.

It is also possible, of course, that the children just cannot understand the dilemma. If this is the case, suggest that they all think about it, and try again some other day.

Absurd Solutions

If a suggestion seems to make no sense, first find out by focused questioning if it is really as strange as it seems. Ask the child for further clarification, and continue questioning until he or she either articulates exactly what is meant by the suggestion or realizes that it does not apply. If this approach fails, restate the problem for the child, asking if this is what he or she understood it to be. If it is, then hold the solution for possible role play. Remember, a seemingly fantastic idea may represent a way that the children might deal with the problem if they faced it in real life.

Several Solutions

If the children consistently suggest several resolutions to decision stories, they are really maturing in their ability to work through dilemmas. When the class suggests more than one alternative ending to a decision story, you must decide the order in which the resolutions are to be enacted. Also, of course, although it is ideal to organize a role play for each of the suggestions, you sometimes have to choose among them. You want to choose solutions that provoke thought among the students. Shaftel and Shaftel (1982) suggest that these be the most socially negative solutions—in other words, the ones that probably seem worst to you. We have followed their suggestion and find that, indeed, these solutions we ourselves would be least likely to adopt contribute most to thoughtful discussion and decision making. It is also worthwhile, at times, to choose solutions that represent a persistent or habitual behavior pattern of your students—ways of acting that they automatically, unthinkingly use when they face problems. In role-playing the behavior, the children may see its consequences as never before.

Use skills of your own and certain simple tactics to make this section of the warm-up easy to handle. First, be a good listener. Ask children to explain what they are thinking, and restate what they say to verify their exact points and to make sure the rest of the students understand, too.

Second, write down the suggestions where both you and the children can see them. Your referring to these public notes as the role play progresses indicates to the children that you respect their thoughts and are organizing the activity around them. It is also a good idea, at the end of the role play, to mention solutions that were not enacted, explaining that you just did not have enough time. Third, avoid suggesting a solution, even if the children are frustratingly silent. If the role-play idea is yours and not theirs, they will feel that they are merely acting out the preference of an authority figure, not reasoning out solutions on their own. And keep the children from evaluating the suggestions in any way at this time. Let the solutions be played out first. Fourth, be patient; give the children time to think about solutions. Often, a little waiting pays off. Finally, move to the action as soon as possible. This part of the session is not meant to be a discussion time.

Getting the Players Ready

Choosing children to play the various characters involves the same balancing act you perform whenever some students must be left out of an activity. The children who make suggestions are often eager to play them out, and they probably should be allowed to take parts. Similarly, children who have ideas about how given characters will act should probably be chosen to take those characters' roles. But all the children eventually should be permitted opportunities to take roles, even if they show little skill at proposing solutions to dilemmas. The role-play experience itself may help develop that skill.

With younger children, try to have each player make a brief statement about the concrete actions his or her character will take. With older children, ask also how they think the characters will feel, and suggest that they guide their actions accordingly. When you ask about these feelings, be sure your tone of voice and facial expressions are value-free. (Asking younger children about characters' feelings may be counterproductive: they tend simply to describe their own feelings, and then they have a hard time stepping into the characters' shoes in role play.)

Next, ask the players to decide whether they will begin the role play where the story left off or pick up the action earlier in the plot. You may need to help younger children make this decision.

Determine, at this point, if the children need props. Props for role play, as for any dramatic play, encourage involvement, make a situation realistic, and offer the players the security of the concrete as the uncertain action unfolds. Props need not be elaborate, however. A desk moved to one corner of the classroom can represent a house. A long piece of paper on the floor can be a creek or a picnic blanket or even a small room. A folded piece of paper can be a toy car, and paper lunch bags can be ice cream or a ball— almost anything. In other words, although props are important, you need not prepare them in advance. Children enjoy choosing props as they move into the action period, and their choices are often very creative.

Preparing Observers

The characters in a role play based on a decision story's resolution are obviously fewer in number than the children in an ordinary class. Nevertheless, all the students must feel that they are part of the action and the solution. It is just as necessary to prepare the observers as it is to assign roles to the players. And, as you might suspect, if you do not prepare observers, the children on the sidelines of the role play are easily distracted and are more likely to behave disruptively.

Be concrete in preparing younger children as observers. You can ask them to report exactly what they see happening, what they think will happen next, or how they think the characters are feeling as the action occurs. Give only one observation assignment to the whole class for each enactment, and describe it simply and directly.

Although you give similar observation assignments to older students, you have the options with them of giving a single observation task to the whole class or giving groups of students different assignments for the same enactment. If you choose to do the latter, for example, you might tell one small group of students to pay attention to the feelings of one character; another small group, the feelings of a different character; and a third group, the likely course the action will take.

The Action Period

Having prepared the children for the action period, you can now step aside and let them spontaneously work through their solutions. As far as the children are concerned, this entire period flows as one experience. For you, however, it has three distinct phases, each of which may require your guidance.

Starting

Children are often so eager to start the role play that they need no encouragement; in fact, they are sometimes so warmed up you may have to cool them down a bit so you can prepare the observers. At other times, a simple "Okay!" or nod of the head is all that is needed.

There are those times, however, when younger children offer no resolutions to a decision story, and you might take a role to get the action going. Because young children generally think their teacher is always right, you must treat your participation delicately. The children should be learning to make decisions on their own and not depend on your thinking. So choose a minor role, act out the decision story with the children, and, as the role play concludes, question the main character to help him or her chart a course.

The Action Itself

The second phase of the action period is the role play itself. As far as possible, stay in the background and let the children take over. After a few experiences, children as young as five are able to work through their solutions with no help from their teacher. Only under these circumstances do children begin to reap the full benefits of the role play. In spontaneously working on their solutions, they begin to realize that, often, for one reason or another, things do not go as they thought they would. They are required to think on their feet and change the planned action accordingly. They are beginning realistically to perceive the consequences of given courses of action. In addition, they may be starting to understand the perspectives of others, a necessary step in the development of a set of personal values.

If it is not possible for you to stay in the background, and you find it necessary to take a role, you still want the children to assume the responsibility for the direction of the role play. In your role as a minor character, you can profitably ask quesions like "What will you do now?" that forward the action.

Stopping

Finally, it is up to you to decide when the action stops. How do you know when to quit? How much is too much; how far, too far? As you and your students become practiced, the time for closure will usually be obvious. There are, of course, specific things to look for, indicators that it is time to move to the debriefing.

Sometimes, you may find that the action is getting out of hand; some children are becoming too physical, or there is silly emoting. Quietly and nonpunitively, simply bring the action to a close.

At other times, children may lose focus and start doing things that have little or no relation to the problem. If the children appear to be trying to clarify the issues through this behavior, let the action continue. See if the children begin to settle themselves into their roles. If not, step in and stop the action.

Sometimes children start repeating their own actions, or simply stop acting altogether. Either behavior is a signal that they have gone as far as they can, and you should move to the debriefing.

Debriefing

Astronauts do it at the end of a mission, football players do it at the end of a game, and we think that, at the end of role play, young children need to debrief, too, and for the same reason. There needs to be a time to review what happened in order better to understand it and extract lessons for the future. Each person involved must become conscious of the meaning of the experience for him or her.

Debriefing After a Single Enactment

In the case of "The Car Crash," suppose the children have just acted out a solution in which Robert has decided to tell the teacher that Brian did indeed break Mitchell's car. In the dramatic action, you have observed that Robert has decided that telling the truth is more important than friendship, that Brian looks defensive and contrite, and that Mitchell would like to act out a physically aggressive response to Brian's mistake.

"Brian," you ask, "how are you feeling now?"

"I hate Robert," he might say.

"Why is that?"

"He promised he wouldn't tell, and he told."

You continue to ask the other players, still in character, about their feelings: "Robert, how about you?"

"I don't know. I think I should have told the teacher, but now I don't have my friend anymore."

"Mitchell, how are you feeling now?"

"Mad."

"Why are you angry?"

"I don't know. I just am."

If the actors want to discuss their feelings or thoughts in greater depth, they should be encouraged to do so. Do not forget, however, that you have given the other children, the observers, responsibilities. As soon as it is possible, open the debriefing to the whole group by reminding the observers of the tasks they were given. Then ask them to report their perceptions of the enactment and what they believe will result from what they saw.

The debriefing of a single enactment usually results in the role play's taking one of two directions. Either in discussion the children suggest ways to continue the present enactment (in which case you select additional participants as necessary, settle individuals into roles, and prepare the observers), or the children suggest no continuation (in which case you organize a different solution suggested during the warm-up or during the discussion after the enactment, and you follow the steps of the warm-up to get this enactment going).

Debriefing of the Whole

Sometimes, even in kindergarten, you have a very verbal child who also possesses a gift for synthesis. He or she might say something like this: "Well, when we acted out Robert telling the teacher, I felt sorry for Brian, because that meant he was going to get in trouble; and, besides, Robert promised he wouldn't tell on him. But then the next time, I got to be Brian, and it didn't feel the same. I felt bad when I didn't get told on and nobody knew who did it. That means somebody else might get in trouble. I think it's better for Robert to tell on Brian."

Sometimes, especially in kindergarten, it takes two or three comments by different children to get this far. However the discussion proceeds, debriefing of the whole set of enactments is important for helping children learn how to make decisions and develop their own values. Even the kindergartner quoted has learned that decision making does not always offer a cut-and-dried happy ending—that there are pros and cons to many alternatives. This same child has learned that even in dilemmas it is possible to make decisions based on personal values. Role-play sessions offer this child a forum for sharing changing ideas with other children, and a chance to think outloud and even act out the alternative ideas.

In this debriefing, help the children examine and evaluate the different solutions they have seen acted out, and then help the children choose which they believe to be most appropriate. Begin by helping the children review each enactment. Taking each suggested solution in turn, ask the children briefly to summarize what happened and how all the characters felt as a result. Structure this discussion to keep the children awake: make it relatively brief, and ask pointed questions like "What happened when Robert told the teacher? How did Brian feel when Robert told? How did Robert feel? What about Mitchell?"

Then ask the children to contribute their ideas and feelings about what might be the most appropriate solution to the problem, and why this solution is the most appropriate as far as they are concerned. Here, again, be nonthreatening and nonjudgmental. Urge the children to reach personal conclusions about what they each would do in such a situation, and why. Although group sharing can be very appropriate at this point, you should make the children aware of the fact that they do not need to articulate their feelings and decisions in front of the others unless they really want to do so. Perhaps invite them to think further on their own, talk with their parents about the issue, or come to you whenever they feel they would like to discuss it. It is not necessary to reach group consensus on a most appropriate solution.

This final phase of the 1-2-3 approach requires the greatest delicacy. Although you want the children to share their ideas if possible, your main goal is to teach them to make their own decisions and develop their own values independently. They can learn from listening to each other. Remember that research in moral development shows that people of all ages are attracted to reasoning at more advanced levels, and be especially encouraged by the fact that the same research shows people are not attracted to levels they have outgrown. So if you have in your class children who speak from a completely egocentric point of view as well as children who are learning to put themselves in others' shoes, it is the latter group that will be influential. You can expect to see growth.

Summary

The following chart summarizes the 1-2-3 approach to role play used with decision stories.

Role Play Used with Decision Stories: The 1-2-3 Approach

1 The Warm-up

A Prepare the children for the decision story
  with a concrete object
  using the children's own experiences
  using your own experiences
  discussing the issues themselves

B Present the decision story
  choose an appropriate story, and practice telling it
  tell the story

C Elicit alternative solutions, and choose those to be acted out
  prepare for no solution, one solution, or absurd solutions
  decide on the order of solutions to be acted out

D Choose and prepare role players
  possibly choose children who proposed solutions or have insight
    into characters
  get a statement of the action to be played out
  choose props, if necessary

E Prepare observers
  emphasize observation of the action as it happens, its predictable
    direction, and characters' feelings

2 The Action Period

A Starting
  allow freedom for spontaneous activity
  take the role of a minor character, only when necessary

B The action itself
  stay in the background
  if taking a minor role, ask directing questions only

C Stopping
  stop when activity has reached a natural conclusion
  stop when the action is out of hand
  stop when players are obviously confused

3 The Debriefing

A At the end of each enactment
  review action from players' and observers' perspectives
  decide on subsequent enactments

B At the end of the role play as a whole
  examine and evaluate each solution
  facilitate the choice of a most appropriate solution
  emphasize the process and reasons, not the choice itself

3

Talking It Through

Techniques for Structured Discussion

In chapter two, we argue that role play is appropriate for young children's developmental levels, that the concreteness of it is sure to help them learn, and that it can engage both their minds and bodies as nothing else can. Why then are we now advocating structured discussion, an alternative approach to addressing values that would appear to offer none of these advantages?

First, we cannot guarantee universal success for role play. Some children may be inhibited by it; discussion is easier for them. Second, discussion may be more appropriate for addressing real-life, on-the-spot problems when role play might lead to a blowup during the action period. Finally, children must begin sometime to learn good discussion techniques. Although they are, in the earliest years, somewhat awkward with group discussion, you can responsibly lower your aim, consider discussion a readiness activity, and enjoy the progress the children make in the development of decision-making and communication skills.

One can engage young children successfully in discussion by making it quite structured, introducing concrete elements into it, and treating it altogether as a directed, rather than free-form, activity. The warm-up, action period, and debriefing of the 1-2-3 approach achieve these goals.

The Warm-up

The warm-up for a structured discussion is shorter and simpler than that for role play. Because no players need be chosen for the action period and no observation tasks assigned, you as the teacher have just two things to do: introduce the decision story to the children, and then share it with them.

Preparation for Listening

Introduce the decision story for structured discussion as you would for role play. Chapter two contains the full discussion that we here review.

Use concrete objects, especially with very young children. Show an object that has some relation to the decision story to the children to capture their interest. Then ask the children to define the object, say how it functions, and possibly discuss their feelings about it. Finally, tell them they will hear a story about an object like the one before them.

Ask children to share their own experiences, telling about situations in their own lives similar to those in the decision story. Emphasize the children's own perceptions and feelings within these experiences. Then invite them to listen to the decision story.

Share your own experiences that roughly parallel the decision story's plot. Focus on the dilemma and on your and others' feelings rather than on how the situation was resolved.

Discuss the abstract issues involved in the decision story's dilemma only when your students are experienced in discussion and when you have all addressed the same issue previously.

Preparing the children to listen in any of these ways motivates them to pay sufficient attention to the decision story to be able to discuss its dilemma with understanding later. Whichever strategy you use, keep it short, probably no more than three or four minutes. Avoid bogging down in preliminary discussion. Keep it simple. When you or the children share experiences from your own lives, emphasize feelings and not details or how it all came out in the end. And be prepared; plan your strategy in advance.

Presentation of the Story

Read, or preferably (especially if the children are younger), tell the story to the children (see chapter two).

Whether you tell or read the decision story in preparation for structured discussion, you can make the story more vivid by using visual aids, pictures

older children, more complex considerations may also be jotted down as suggested.

Use the informal method when the class needs a change of pace, or when only one or two children raise their hands with suggested endings for a decision story. To keep the discussion moving, just deal with the first suggestion; other solutions probably will occur to the children.

The Debriefing

As with role play, the debriefing with structured discussion is the time when the class tries to decide the most appropriate way of solving a decision story's problem. It is also the time when the issues implicit in the problem are considered explicitly.

Considering the Decision

Now move the discussion to a comparison of all possible consequences so that the children can judge the alternative suggested courses of action.

Review the discussion so far. Point to each alternative on the chart, say what it is, and ask the children to restate its likely consequences (the illustrations or notes on the chart will help them do so). This entire review should not take long.

Next, evaluate the consequences in relation to each other. Start by asking the children to examine each alternative in terms of the relative numbers of its positive and negative consequences. In doing this, the students are, in a simplified manner, weighing the alternative with respect to the feelings it might produce. Next, ask the children to compare the numbers of positive and negative consequences of each alternative to the numbers for each of the others. It should be obvious to them that some alternatives have greater merit, or at least produce greater happiness. If they do not see this, point it out to them.

Now, decision making is no mere numbers game, and right action does not always produce the greatest measurable happiness, as adults know. So, at this point, help the children look at the circumstances surrounding the alternatives. Ask them why, other than because of the feelings it would produce, a given alternative may or may not be acceptable. You might also ask if there could be any reason that a particular alternative with many positive personal consequences might not be acceptable.

Suppose, for example, that a class discussing "The Car Crash" has found that there are the most positive personal consequences for the alternative in which Robert decides to tell the teacher. Then you might ask if, even though this alternative would make many people happy, anyone still thinks it is not a good idea. One child might argue that it would not be acceptable because Robert had promised Brian he would not tell. The child might say that, as far as he or she is concerned, keeping promises is the most important thing. This child would be articulating an important personal value that overrides considerations of feelings.

Finally, ask the children to choose what they consider to be the most appropriate alternative, and to decide why it is most appropriate. Remember, at issue here is a somewhat delicate question: should children announce their final decisions or keep them to themselves?

You can appropriately have the children make their decisions public when you realize that different children will make different choices and that these choices will be accepted by the others without derogatory comment. Public statement is also appropriate when it appears that there is true group consensus in favor of one alternative.

Forgo public announcement, on the other hand, if you think a child is on the verge of a minority decision that will be strongly rejected by others. Similarly, do not ask for open statements if you think that some children might feel coerced to go along with the majority. Do not let this part of the discussion turn into an election or a popularity contest; each child must make a true personal moral choice.

When you feel that publicity is inappropriate, you might ask the children to sit quietly and think what their choices would be. If they are old enough to write, you might ask them to write the choices on pieces of paper to hand to you. You could also encourage the children to discuss their choices with you or their parents later.

Addressing the Abstract Issues

Older children often are able to address values abstractly during the debriefing. They can look at long-range consequences and discuss social issues per se apart from the context of the decision story.

A discussion of abstract issues could be a natural extension of the evaluation of consequences in the debriefing. Recall the child who disagreed with the rest of the class concerning the outcome of "The Car Crash," on the grounds that, although telling the teacher had the least number of negative consequences, keeping a promise was simply more important. You could reintroduce this argument when it seems appropriate, probably now, toward the end of the debriefing. You might say, "Someone mentioned that Robert shouldn't tell the teacher because he'd be breaking a promise. Let's talk about the idea of keeping promises." Then help the children examine promise keeping from a variety of perspectives. You could consider questions such as whether one should always keep a promise and why promises might sometimes be broken.

Another way to approach abstract issues in the debriefing is to focus on the issues raised by the decision story, generally discussing the children's ideas and feelings about them outside the story's context. Be aware of the values in conflict in the story, and formulate questions directed at probing the limits of each child's support of a given value.

Whether you use the children's own arguments as a starting point or go straight to the abstract issues within the decision story, your questions will sound the same. Here are some suggestions based on the seven values at issue in the decision stories in chapter four. You will notice that some of the questions involve more than one value at a time.

1   Authority: Should you always do something someone older asks you to do? How about someone who's bigger? When are some times you might not do what an older person tells you to?

2   Friendship: Should you always do something a friend asks you to do? Should you share more with a good friend than with someone you don't know so well? Is it more important to keep a promise you made to a friend than to someone else? What is a friend, anyway?

3   Promises: Should you always keep a promise? Why is it important to keep them?

4   Property: Should you always keep your hands off other people's things? How do you know when you should? When is it okay for people to touch and use your things?

5   Rules: Why is it important to obey rules? Who makes up the rules? Should you always obey rules?

6   Sharing: Is it always good to share? How do you know how much of something you should share? Is it ever okay to keep everything for yourself?

7   Truth: Are there times when it's okay not to tell the truth? Why is it important to tell the truth to your teacher [parent, friend]?

Summary

Structured discussion offers an alternative to role play that, for the youngest children, is a readiness activity for more mature discussions later. The following chart summarizes the 1-2-3 approach to structured discussion used with decision stories.

Structured Discussion Used with Decision Stories: The 1-2-3 Approach

1   The Warm-up

A   **Prepare the children for the decision story**
with a concrete object
using the children's own experiences
using your own experiences
discussing the issues themselves

    B **Present the decision story**
          choose an appropriate story, and practice telling it
          tell the story

2 The Action Period

    A **Using the systematic method**
          list all alternatives first
          illustrate alternatives on a chart
          regroup alternatives if appropriate
          reorder alternatives if necessary
          discuss each in order, focusing on feelings
          enter consequences on positive or negative side of chart

    B **Using the informal method**
          elicit consequences of each alternative as it is presented
          enter consequences on positive or negative side of chart

3 The Debriefing

    A **Consider the decision**
          review alternatives and their consequences
          evaluate alternatives and consequences in relation to each other
          choose the most appropriate resolution

    B **Discuss abstract issues**
          using ideas the children have raised in discussion
          using issues inherent in the decision story

4

Decision Stories

Materials for Role Play and Discussion

This chapter contains thirty-four decision stories, most of which you can use as is or adapt in one way or another to suit your class. We hope they also give you ideas for new decision stories to develop yourself with the aid of chapter five, "Making Your Own."

You can use most of the stories with children at several grade levels. The grade levels for which the stories are appropriate are noted in the upper left-hand corner above each story; the stories appear in order of rising grade levels.

Also noted in the upper left-hand corner above each decision story are the issues the story raises. On page vi and again below, just before the decision stories themselves, is a chart that can help you choose stories to use with your students. The chart lists each decision story, the issues it raises, the grade levels for which it is appropriate, and the page on which it appears. You can use this chart to choose stories on the basis of issues or grade level.

Modify stories to suit your students. For example, we wrote "Who Takes the Cake?" for third graders and presented it to a third grade class as it appears here. When the story later was used with second graders, the bike ride in it was changed to a trip to a park next to the school. Finally, when the story was adapted for first graders, the trip was changed to a stay in the park, with Barbara's mother dropping the children off and arranging to pick them up in an hour. The mother also made Barbara's lunch for her. These changes were all that was necessary to adapt a third grade story for earlier grades.

Incidentally, during the experimental altering of "Who Takes the Cake?" we were struck (as we frequently are) by the creativity of young children's reasoning in the face of a problem, and it was a first grade group that surprised us most. Remember, be ready for anything the children have to offer; they frequently have ideas that have not occurred to you.

Suggestions for use accompany each story. First we suggest warm-up strategies. Next we print the story itself. Then, with stories appropriate for older children, we include questions about abstract issues that can be used in the debriefing. Then come pictures of major characters and objects to use as you chart alternative suggestions and consequences in structured discussion. (We do not recommend the pictures for role play; let the players visualize their own characters.) Feel free to duplicate the pictures. The faces are expressionless so that you can modify them with a pen or marker to represent your children's suggestions.

As you prepare to use the stories, you might find it helpful to refer to the charts at the ends of chapters two and three to refresh you memory of techniques to use with role play and structured discussion respectively.

Have patience. Your students' first attempts at structured discussion or role play may show evidence of very little progress in their reasoning, and you may feel that nothing is being accomplished. Progress comes as you and the children gain experience. We are sure you will then take delight in the growing abilities of your children to think, reason, and discuss.

Duplicating the Illustrations

Remove the pages with illustrations on them from the book. Make photocopies. Then cut up the photocopies, not the pages themselves. (Keep the pages as masters for future duplication.)

Decision Stories

TITLE	ISSUES	GRADES	PAGE
The Ice Cream Is Melting	authority, rules	K	44
Should Travis Tell?	friendship, truth	K	47
Come On, Kevin, Just This Once!	authority, sharing	K, 1	49
But You Promised!	friendship, promises, sharing	K, 1	52
The Car Crash	authority, friendship, promises, property, truth	K, 1	55
Robby's New Friends	friendship, property, truth	K, 1, 2	58
A Muddy Mess	rules, truth	K, 1, 2, 3	61
Red Rover, Red Rover	property, rules	K, 1, 2, 3	63
The Missing Candy Bar	friendship, sharing, truth	K, 1, 2, 3	66
Cookies or Cupcakes?	authority, sharing	K, 1, 3	68
Deke's Secret	property, sharing, truth	K, 1, 3	71
Hands Off the Cookie Jar!	promises, rules	1, 2, 3	74
If He Hits You, Hit Him Back!	authority, rules	1, 2, 3	77
Mrs. Jeffrey's Surprise	authority, sharing	1, 3	80
The Haunted House	authority, friendship	1, 2, 3	83
Grandma Likes Baseball	friendship, promises	1, 2, 3	86
Don't Worry, We'll Be Careful!	friendship, property, sharing	1, 2, 3	89
Trouble in the Tree House	authority, promises, rules, truth	2, 3	92
Tattletale, Tattletale!	friendship, rules	2, 3	95
Mean Ronnie	authority, property	2, 3	98
Melinda's Biggest Kick	promises, property	2, 3	100
The Bike Trick	property, sharing	2, 3	103
The Dollar, the Candy, and the Poor Boy	friendship, sharing	2, 3	106
One More Goal To Win!	friendship, promises, sharing	2, 3, 3+	109
Whose Money Is It, Anyway?	authority, truth	3, 3+	112
Just Don't Bug Me Anymore!	promises, property, truth	3, 3+	114
Mrs. Crabby	property, truth	3, 3+	116
Max's Mess	authority, friendship, promises	3, 3+	119
Abby's First Job	authority, friendship, promises	3, 3+	121
Stephanie and Star	authority, friendship	3, 3+	123
Last One In Is a Rotten Fried Egg!	friendship, rules	3, 3+	125
The Ice Cream Special	rules, sharing	3, 3+	127
Who Takes the Cake?	promises, sharing	3, 3+	129
Adrian's Sunday	friendship, promises	3, 3+	132

Grade: K
Issues: authority, rules

The Ice Cream Is Melting

Warm-up

(*Children's experiences*) ASK "How many of you have rules at home? What are some of the rules you have at your house?"

OR (*Teacher's experience*) SHARE a rule your family had when you were a child. Explain why your family had this rule.

THEN SAY "This is a story about a boy whose family had some rules. One of those rules caused him a problem one day. Let's listen."

The Ice Cream Is Melting

Tony was home alone for just a little while. Usually his mom and his big sister, Elena, were there. But they had wanted to go shopping, and Tony hated to shop. Mom had said he could stay home by himself because it would be for only an hour, but he was to remember the rules.

Tony knew the rules, all right. Number one was that he shouldn't do anything dangerous in the kitchen like using a knife or anything electric. Number two was that he should stay in the house. And number three was that he shouldn't let anybody else in the house.

When his mom and sister left for the store, Tony began playing with the Space Race game he'd gotten for his birthday. He was having a good time, not missing anybody at all, when the doorbell rang. For a minute Tony forgot that he was alone, and he ran to the door. Just as he started to open it, he remem-

bered the rule about not letting anybody in. So he called, "Who's there?"

"Tony," said a familiar voice, "is that you? This is Mrs. Morgan from down the street."

"Oh," said Tony, "I'm sorry, Mrs. Morgan, but I can't let anybody in. My mom isn't home."

"Oh, Tony, honey," Mrs. Morgan said, "I have a problem. We made some ice cream and we had too much, so I brought some over for your family. It needs to go in the freezer right away, or it will melt."

"I don't know what to do," Tony told her. "I told mom I'd obey the rules, and not letting anybody in is one of the rules."

"And you're a really good boy to obey the rules," Mrs. Morgan answered. "But you know me, Tony, and you know nothing will happen if you open the door. This ice cream needs to be taken care of right away, dear."

Tony didn't know what to do.

Action Period   *The following pictures may be duplicated.*

The Ice Cream Is Melting

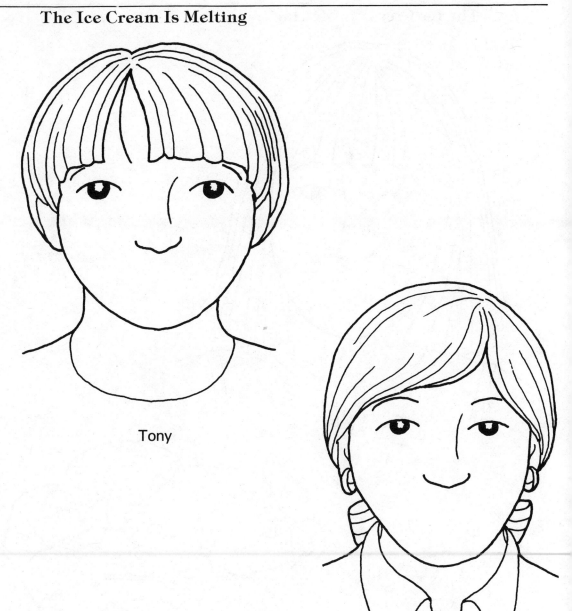

Tony

Mrs. Morgan

The Ice Cream Is Melting

Mother

Ice Cream

Grade: K
Issues: friendship, truth

Warm-up

(*Children's experiences*) ASK "How many of you have ever tried to ride a two-wheeled bike? What happened?"

OR (*Concrete object*) SHOW two pictures, one a bicycle and one a tricycle. ASK "What is the difference between a bicycle and a tricycle? Which one is harder to ride?"

THEN SAY "Today we're going to hear a story about a boy who is just beginning to learn to ride a two-wheeled bike."

Should Travis Tell?

Should Travis Tell?

Travis had a perfectly good tricycle. It was red and shiny, there were hardly any scratch marks on it, and it was just the right size for him. But that's not what he wanted. Travis wanted a real two-wheeled bike like the one his friend George had. Travis had tried to ride George's bike a couple of times, and it wasn't easy, but he could stay on a little bit. Travis just knew that if he had his own bike he could stay on for sure.

One day Travis walked over to George's house. They were good friends and played at each other's houses a lot. "Can I try the bike a little bit?" Travis asked.

"Well," said George, and he seemed to be thinking about it.

"I'll be real careful, I promise," Travis said.

"Well, okay," George said. "But you'd better not let anything happen to it, because it's my favorite toy in the whole world."

So Travis got on and started to ride around the yard. He was doing pretty well, too, when George's mother called, "George, come here a minute."

"I'll be right back," George said to Travis.

Travis took off on the bike again, and everything was going fine when, suddenly, *bang*, he hit a rock. The bike tumbled over and Travis went with it. He picked himself up and discovered he wasn't hurt at all. Then he picked up the bike and saw a bad scratch all along the side that had hit the rock.

He was really scared about what would happen when George came back out. He quickly put the bike back in the garage where it belonged, leaning it against a wagon. When George came out, Travis said, "I got tired of riding the bike. Let's go over to my house and play soccer for a while."

Although they had a good time playing soccer, Travis kept thinking about the ugly scratch. It made him feel bad inside that he hurt his friend's toy.

The next day George came over to Travis's house. He was riding the bike and didn't look happy at all.

"Look at this," he said, and pointed to the ugly scratch on the bike. "My bike fell over in the garage. My parents are really going to be angry with me, and I'm really going to get it. I don't know what I'm going to do."

A lot of thoughts ran through Travis's head. He knew that if he told George what really happened to the bike, George might not be his friend anymore. He also knew that if he didn't tell the truth, George would probably be punished.

He didn't want to lose his friend, and he didn't want George to get into trouble. What could he do?

Action Period   *The following pictures may be duplicated.*

Should Travis Tell?

Travis

George

George's Parents

Grades: K, 1
Issues: authority, sharing

Grades: K, 1
Issues: authority, sharing

Come On, Kevin, Just This Once!

Warm-up

(*Children's experiences*) ASK "Do any of you have toys at home that could break easily? Are you afraid to let anyone play with them? Do you wish you could share them or do you like keeping them just to yourself?"

OR (*Concrete object*) Bring to class an intricately made, delicate toy like the cars in Kevin's story.

ASK "This is a beautiful toy, isn't it? Have you ever owned a breakable toy like this that you wanted to share, but you were afraid to, because it might break? Can you tell us about it?"

THEN SAY "Listen closely now while I tell you the story of a boy who had some very breakable toys that he couldn't share."

Come On, Kevin, Just This Once!

Sometimes Kevin's grandmother gave him special presents when he visited her. Kevin's favorite was a set of three little race cars that she had given him last Saturday. He liked them because you could open the doors and move the steering wheels, and they had little men you could take in and out. As you can probably tell, Kevin had to be careful not to lose the little men or break the tiny steering wheels. In fact, his grandmother said to him, "Kevin, these cars are really special and they cost a lot of money. Take very good care of them. I think this is one set of toys you'd better just play with yourself, just to make sure they don't get hurt."

So Kevin played with the cars only at home. One morning he played with them so long he almost missed the school bus. "Hurry," his mother called, "you're going to miss the bus!"

Without really thinking about it, Kevin put the cars into his jacket pockets, grabbed his lunch, and raced out the door to the bus stop. He didn't think about the cars again until it was time to go out on the playground after lunch. On the way out, Kevin stuck his hands in his pockets, and there the cars were. Oh, how he wanted to play with them! But he had a feeling he'd better not, because then some-body else might want to play with them, too.

But all the kids he liked to play with seemed to be going off to play kickball. Kevin didn't like kickball much, so he just stood around for a few minutes wondering what to do. Then, since nobody was around at all, Kevin took the cars out of his pockets and started playing with them on the grass. He was having a good time, too, when he suddenly realized that someone was standing in front of him. Two someones in fact.

"Hey," said Kevin's friend Richard, "those are sure great-looking cars."

"Yeah," said Wanda, who was standing there too. "I especially like the red one. Could I see it for a minute?"

Kevin started to put the cars back in his pocket and said, "No, I'm just supposed to play with these myself."

"Aw, come on," said Richard. "I'm your best friend. You know I won't hurt them. There are three cars and three kids. We could have a good time playing."

"Sure," said Wanda. "I'd be careful, too."

"Well," thought Kevin, "maybe just this once. I know they're careful kids. They really are." But then he thought about his grandmother spending all that money and telling him not to let other kids play with the cars. He really didn't know what to do.

Action Period *The following pictures may be duplicated.*

Come On, Kevin, Just This Once!

Kevin

Wanda

Come On, Kevin, Just This Once!

Richard

Cars

Grades: K, 1
Issues: friendship, promises, sharing

But You Promised!

Warm-up

(*Concrete object*) SHOW a playground ball. ASK "You all know what this is, don't you? Do you ever have to wait your turn before you can play with it? How does that make you feel?"

OR (*Children's experiences*) ASK "Do you ever have to wait for any of the toys or equipment at recess? How do you feel while you're waiting?"

THEN SAY "Today we're going to hear about some children just like you who had to wait their turns at recess. We're especially going to hear about two of those children. Listen carefully, because they had a problem that you might have been able to help them with."

But You Promised!

Megan had just gotten a large red ball for her birthday. It was called a playground ball, and you could play soccer or dodgeball or kickball with it. She decided to take it to school to use at recess. It seemed there were never enough balls to go around at recess time.

Megan got to school a little early, and only one other child was there. It was Ben, a boy nobody played with very often. She had been hoping that one of her good friends would be there to show the ball to, but Ben thought it looked like a really good one.

"Hey," he said, "I'd really like to try out that ball. Could I borrow it at recess time?"

Megan wasn't sure she wanted him to, but she didn't know what to say, so she just answered, "Okay."

"Promise?" Ben asked.

"Yeah, okay," Megan said. She could see that Ben was very happy that she would let

him play with her ball.

When recess came, Megan wished she hadn't said okay. By then all her friends were there, and they all wanted to play with the ball. They all had even agreed that they could share the ball, and everybody would play dodgeball together.

Just then, however, up came Ben, straight for Megan and the ball. "Here I am," he said, and he had a big smile on his face. "Don't forget I'm going to play with the ball."

"Oh, come on, Ben," said one of the other kids. "We want to play dodgeball with it. And Megan's our friend."

"She promised me," Ben said, "didn't you Megan? You promised me, didn't you?"

Megan looked at her friends. She was afraid they might not like her if she didn't share the ball with them.

"Well, didn't you?" Ben asked again.

Action Period   *The following pictures may be duplicated.*

But You Promised!

Megan

Ben

But You Promised!

Children

Ball

Grades: K, 1
Issues: authority, friendship, promises, property, truth

The Car Crash

Warm-up

(*Concrete object*) Bring a small red car to class and place it in front of you. ASK "This is a nice car, isn't it? How would you feel if it were yours and somebody broke it? Suppose you were the person who broke it, but you didn't do it on purpose. How would you feel?"

OR (*Children's experiences*) ASK "Can anyone tell us about a new toy you have? How would you feel if your new toy broke?"

THEN SAY "I'm going to tell you a story today about some boys who had just these problems."

The Car Crash

Robert was playing in the block corner, building a small house, all by himself. And he was watching Mitchell and Brian build a garage with some bigger blocks.

Robert heard Mitchell say, "I'm tired of building this garage. I'm going to the easel and paint."

"Okay," said Brian, "but will you leave your red racing car here? I want to play with it."

"Sure," Mitchell answered, "but take good care of it, because I got it for my birthday." Then Mitchell went to the easel.

Robert kept on building his small house, and he kept on watching Brian build the garage. He saw Brian start to zoom the red racing car around and over the garage. Suddenly the car crashed into a block wall, and a car door fell off.

"Uh-oh," Robert said. "Mitchell's going to be mad at you."

Brian looked very worried. "Don't tell on me," he begged. "I didn't *mean* to break it!"

Robert thought for a moment. Brian was his good friend, and he didn't want him to get in trouble. "Okay," he said, "I won't tell."

Brian took the red racing car and put it in Mitchell's cubby. He tried to make the door look as though it was still on.

After a while, the teacher said it was time to clean up.

"Where's my racing car?" Mitchell asked Brian.

"I put it in your cubby," Brian answered.

Mitchell went to his cubby and took the car out. The door fell to the floor with a clatter.

"Oh, no!" Mitchell cried. "What did you do to my car, Brian?"

"Nothing," said Brian. "I didn't break it."

Mitchell took his red car to the teacher. "Somebody broke my car," he said.

The teacher gathered all the children around her. "Who broke Mitchell's car?" she asked.

"I didn't," said everybody—even Brian.

Mitchell looked at Brian. "I'll bet you did it!" he yelled.

"I did not!" Brian yelled back.

Robert looked at them both. Then he looked at the teacher. She seemed very angry. First he remembered that he'd promised his friend Brian not to tell. He knew Brian hadn't broken the car on purpose.

Then the teacher said, "If someone knows what really happened, please say so. It's very important to tell the truth."

"Oh, dear," thought Robert, "what should I do now?"

Action Period   *The following pictures may be duplicated.*

The Car Crash

Brian

Robert

The Car Crash

Teacher

Mitchell

Car

Grades: K, 1, 2
Issues: friendship, property, truth

Warm-up

(*Children's experiences*) ASK "How many of you didn't know many people when you first came to this school? How did you feel not having many friends?"

OR (*Children's experiences*) ASK "What are some ways kids use to make other kids their friends?" If

Robby's New Friends

children do not suggest asking other children to play, then mention this alternative.

THEN SAY "Here's a story about Robby, who didn't have many friends. Let's listen to what happened when he was just about to get some."

Robby's New Friends

Robby was a very shy and very quiet boy. Nobody seemed to want to play with him much because he was so quiet. He had one good friend, whose name was Todd. Todd liked to play with Robby, but he also liked to play with a lot of other boys in their class. All the boys liked to play with Todd, too. This was good, because whenever Robby was with Todd, the boys would let Robby play with them. They were nice to him because they didn't want to get Todd mad. But if Todd wasn't around, they wouldn't play with Robby, and he felt lonely. He was glad that Todd was his friend.

One morning Robby got to school early. That meant he could play on the playground for a few minutes. He looked around for Todd, but Todd wasn't there yet. Some of the other boys were, though, and they called Robby to come play dodgeball with them. It was the very first time they had ever asked Robby to play with them, and he ran to their circle feeling very, very happy.

Robby looked at the ball they were using. "Where'd you get that ball? Isn't it Todd's?" he asked.

"Oh, he forgot it yesterday," one of them said. "It's okay, though. He won't mind if we use it."

Robby wondered if it really was okay. Then another boy said, "Sure, Todd won't mind."

So Robby decided not to worry, and he joined in the game.

Suddenly, the ball bounced out of the game, over the fence, and into the street. The boys knew they shouldn't run into the street, so they all watched to see what would happen. Just then, a car came along and ran right over Todd's ball! There was a loud pop and that was the end of the ball.

The boys all looked at each other. "I don't think we should tell Todd," said one.

"He'll be mad if we don't," Robby said.

"He won't be mad if he doesn't know about it," someone else said.

The biggest boy suggested, "Why don't we make a deal? Let's all agree not to tell Todd and he'll just think he lost the ball. Because we really didn't *mean* to hurt the ball, did we?"

All the boys except Robby agreed that this was a good idea. Robby thought it was better to tell Todd. He looked at the boys and they looked at him. The biggest boy stared very hard at Robby. "We're all going to shake hands on this deal, and you'd better, too, Robby, or we won't play with you again."

Robby looked at them all shaking hands together, and he wanted to be their friend. But then he thought about Todd. He wanted to be Todd's friend, too.

What could Robby do?

Action Period   *The following pictures may be duplicated.*

Red Rover, Red Rover

Grades: K, 1, 2, 3
Issues: property, rules

Warm-up

(*Children's experiences*) ASK "Are there any places around school or around your neighborhood where you're not allowed to go? Why not? Did you ever feel as though you needed to go there anyway? Can you tell about it?"

OR (*Concrete object*) Bring a large ball to class. ASK "Sometimes balls roll away from you pretty fast, don't they? Is there any place you shouldn't chase them if they do get away?"

THEN SAY "Our story today is about a soccer ball that got away, and it rolled right into a place that nobody was allowed to go. Let's see if we can think of a way to get it back."

Red Rover, Red Rover

Next to Kelly's school was a big field where everyone played lots of games during P.E. On the other side of the field was a forest with many trees. The school had a rule that children could play in the field but not in the forest. There were even some signs right at the edge of the forest that read, "No one is allowed in the forest." The children were always good about obeying that rule. It looked a little spooky in there, anyway.

One day Kelly's class was playing soccer out in the field. When the bell for the next class rang, the coach asked Kelly to bring in the ball. All the other kids lined up and started in. Kelly went after the ball, but it was way at the other end of the field. As she was running toward it, she saw something big and reddish brown come running out of the woods straight toward the ball. It was Kelly's dog, Red Rover! Just as Kelly got to the ball, Red Rover gave a big bark and pushed the ball away. The other kids and the coach were almost back to the building by that time, but they all saw what happened. It made them laugh.

"We'll see you inside, Kelly," called the coach. "You'd better tell your dog to go home." Then they all disappeared inside the building.

Kelly said, "Go home, Red," but her dog just bounced around a little and pushed the ball again. "I said, go home!" Kelly reached for the ball, and this time she was so mad at Red Rover that she kicked the ball by mistake when she went to get it. That was too bad, because the ball went right into the woods with Red Rover running after it.

"Oh, no," Kelly said. "There goes the ball." And as she said that, Red Rover gave it one more push so it went farther into the woods, and then he trotted on toward home the way he should have in the first place.

Now Kelly didn't know what to do. Coach wanted her to get the ball, and it was time for her next class. She knew she'd better hurry or the teacher would be angry. But right in front of Kelly was a sign that said, "No one is allowed in the forest."

Debriefing *Questions for possible discussion:*

1 Why do we have rules about not going in the forest or running out into the street? Why is it important to obey them? Are there any times when you wouldn't obey these rules?

2 Why is it important to take good care of the things that belong to school? What will happen if we don't?

Action Period *The following pictures may be duplicated.*

Red Rover, Red Rover

Kelly

Coach

Red Rover, Red Rover

Teacher

Ball

Grades: K, 1, 2, 3
Issues: friendship, sharing, truth

The Missing Candy Bar

Warm-up

(*Children's experiences*) ASK "How many of you have been trick-or-treating? Did you ever get something so special you just didn't want to share it with anybody? Can you tell about it?"

OR (*Concrete object*) If it is close to Halloween, bring one large candy bar to class and enough small pieces so that each child can have one after the entire role play or discussion is finished. During role play the candy can be used as a prop. ASK "Why does this candy make me think of Halloween? Have you ever gotten some that was so special you just didn't want to share it with anybody? Can you tell about it?"

THEN SAY "Our story today is about a girl who felt just the way you did about sharing that special candy."

The Missing Candy Bar

Ken and Karen were twins. Even though Ken was a boy and Karen was a girl, they looked a lot alike. They also did a lot of things together. They shared most of their toys, not because anybody made them, but because they just liked to share with each other. That's the way twins are.

Halloween was coming. Ken and Karen had been planning to go trick-or-treating with all their friends, but when the big day came, Ken didn't feel well and he had to stay home from school. That night he didn't feel well either, so mom and dad made him stay home from trick-or-treating.

"Don't worry," Karen said, "I'll tell all the people you're sick and ask them to give me a double amount." Ken thought that was a really nice idea and thanked Karen for thinking of it.

Karen went out with their friends then, and at each house she told the people about Ken's being sick, and each time the people were friendly and gave her a double amount of whatever treat they had. You can imagine how heavy Karen's trick-or-treat bag was getting!

Everything went well until the kids came to a small brick house down the block. Every year the lady who lived there gave everyone a very large chocolate bar. It was the biggest treat

anybody gave, and it was Karen's favorite.

"Could I have one for my sick brother?" Karen asked.

The lady looked at her for a minute. "I think one will be enough," she said. "These are very big bars, and I don't have too many to give out."

Karen thanked her for the one chocolate bar, but she felt pretty disappointed. As the kids walked away, one of them said, "I don't think she believes your brother is home sick."

"You're probably right," Karen said. Well, when she got home, Karen took the big bag of candy to Ken's room. But just before she did that, Karen did one other thing. Very quietly, she went into her own room and put the big candy bar in her desk drawer. Karen thought she should have the candy because she was the one who did all the walking. Then she went to see Ken.

"Wow!" Ken said when Karen brought in the big, heavy, full bag. "We got a lot of stuff, didn't we?" Then the two of them split up everything so they each had the same amount.

When they were all finished, Ken looked puzzled. "Didn't you get one of those big candy bars this year? From the lady in the brick house?"

What is Karen going to say now?

Debriefing *Questions for possible discussion:*

1 Why is sharing a good thing to do?

2 How do you know how much you should share with someone? Is it more important to share with a brother or sister than with other people?

Action Period *The following pictures may be duplicated.*

The Missing Candy Bar

Karen

Ken

Chocolate Bar

Grades: K, 1, 3
Issues: authority, sharing

Cookies or Cupcakes?

Warm-up

(*Children's experiences*) SAY "I noticed that the cafeteria has [had] ———— for dessert today. What do [did] you think of it? Some of us like some things better than others, don't we?"

OR (*Children's experiences*) ASK "Does the person who fixes your lunch ever put things into it that you don't like to eat?"

THEN SAY "This is a story about a boy who sometimes liked the desserts his mother put in his lunch and sometimes didn't."

Cookies or Cupcakes?

Amos was hurrying to get ready for school. His mother handed him his lunch and said, "Now, be careful and don't squash it. And don't peek into it, either, until lunchtime. There's a special surprise in there for you."

Amos promised he wouldn't. When it was lunchtime, Amos sat down next to his friend Randall and opened the bag.

"Oh, no," he said. "Look what my mom's surprise is. Carrot cookies. Again! I'm so tired of these."

Randall looked and said, "Yeah, well, I wish my mom would bake me some cookies. I've got those chocolate cupcakes from the grocery store again."

"Gee, you're lucky," Amos said.

"I guess," Randall said. "I'm just tired of them, that's all. Hey! I've got an idea. Why don't we share our desserts with each other? I'll give you my chocolate cupcakes, and you give me your carrot cookies."

At first Amos thought that was a great idea. Then he remembered that his mom had baked the cookies especially for him. He was sure that when he got home, she'd ask him how he liked the surprise.

"Well?" said Randall. "Are you going to trade or not?"

Debriefing   *Questions for possible discussion:*

1   How important is it for you to obey your parents?

2   Is it always a good idea to share? Are there times when you shouldn't share?

3   Are there some things you'd share and some things you wouldn't share? Why would you share some things and not other things?

Action Period   *The following pictures may be duplicated.*

Cookies or Cupcakes?

Amos

Randall

Cookies or Cupcakes?

Mother

Cookies

Cupcakes

Grades: K, 1, 3
Issues: property, sharing, truth

Warm-up

(*Children's experiences*) ASK "How many of you have ever really wanted something that somebody else had, but couldn't have it? How did you feel?"

OR (*Teacher's experience*) SHARE a time when you were a child and wanted but could not have something that a sibling or friend had. Emphasize how you felt in this situation.

Deke's Secret

THEN SAY "Deke thought he really wanted something his brother had. This caused him a problem, though. Let's listen carefully to see if we can help him solve the problem."

Deke's Secret

Deke knew just where his brother Danny had hidden that big bag of potato chips. It was under Danny's bed behind the box of trucks and cars. Deke really wanted some of those chips, too, but Danny wouldn't give him any. Danny said he'd bought them with his own money, and Deke couldn't have any. Period. But Deke had been watching very closely the last time Danny had gone into his room, and he saw Danny put the bag under the bed.

"He's mean," Deke thought to himself. "He's mean not to give me any, but I'll fix him. I'm going to get some anyway!" So Deke waited until Danny went to a friend's house, and he sneaked into Danny's room. The bag of potato chips was right where he thought it was. Deke put it under his shirt and went out very quietly.

"I'd better eat these out on the back porch," he thought. "Danny might come home early." So Deke took the bag out to the back porch and sat down. He looked all around him. No, there wasn't anybody in sight. He started to take a chip out and suddenly stopped. It had just occurred to Deke for the first time that he was stealing!

"Gosh!" he said out loud. "Danny's mean, all right, but I guess I shouldn't take them. I sure don't want to steal." Deke was thinking so hard about what he had done that he didn't see his friends Kim and James walking up.

"Hi, Deke!" they said together.

Deke looked up in surprise. He tried to hide the bag behind his back. "Oh, hi!" he said.

"What's that behind your back?" Kim asked.

"It's a bag of potato chips," James said. "I saw it before he tried to hide it."

"Well?" asked Kim. "Aren't you going to share some with us?"

"I can't," Deke replied.

"How come?" they asked. "We're your friends, aren't we? Don't you want to share with your friends?"

Deke wanted his friends to like him. But if he shared the potato chips instead of putting them back, it would be stealing. If he told them the truth, they might think he was really bad for taking them. He didn't want anybody to know about that. He just wanted to put the bag back and forget he made that mistake.

"Well?" Kim asked again. "Aren't you going to share?"

Debriefing   *Questions for possible discussion:*

1   Is it ever okay not to tell your friends the truth? Why? When?

2   Which is more important, telling the truth or having friends? Why?

3   Is it ever okay not to share something? Why? When?

4   If you were going to share something, would you rather share it with your brother or sister or with your friends? Why?

Action Period   *The following pictures may be duplicated.*

Deke's Secret

Deke

Kim

James

Deke's Secret

Danny

Potato Chips

Grades: 1, 2, 3
Issues: promises, rules

Hands Off the Cookie Jar!

Warm-up

(*Children's experiences*) ASK "How many of you have big brothers or big sisters? Do they ever boss you around? How does that make you feel?"

OR (*Teacher's experience*) If you had a big brother or sister, SHARE briefly how it felt to be in the junior position. You might cite an illustrative incident.

THEN SAY "In our story today, Alex had a big sister named Mary who liked to tell him what to do, too. Sometimes it caused him problems with his own plans, as we'll see."

Hands Off the Cookie Jar!

Alex liked to play football with José, who lived next door. But José was older than Alex, and sometimes he was just too busy, or he wanted to play with his older friends instead.

One day, Alex was out in his yard kicking the football around, wishing for somebody to play with, when he saw José.

"Hey, José," he called, "want to kick the football around some with me?"

"I can't," answered José. "I've got homework." Alex thought that maybe José just didn't want to play because José was so much better than Alex, and it was probably boring for him. Alex had an idea then. He thought he might know how to get José to play with him. "Hey," he said. "You really like the chocolate chip cookies my mom makes, don't you?"

"Boy, I sure do," José said

"Well, I'll make a deal with you," Alex answered. "If you'll play football with me for, oh, just about ten minutes or so, I'll take you into the kitchen to get some cookies mom just made today."

"You sure she won't mind?" José asked.

"Naw, I don't think so. Besides, she's not home now anyway, so it doesn't matter."

So José agreed to play. Alex thought it seemed they had just started when José was saying, "Okay, time's up. Let's go get those cookies you promised."

The two boys went through Alex's back door and into the kitchen. There in the cookie jar were plenty of freshly baked, very big and soft chocolate chip cookies. Alex picked up the jar and held it so that José could choose some.

"Boy, those smell good," José said. "I'll take three."

A new voice interrupted, "Oh, no, you won't!" It was Alex's big sister, Mary. She had just come into the kitchen. "No, you won't take those cookies. Look at the time!"

Alex and José looked at the clock on the kitchen wall. It said 5:30. "It's 5:30," Alex said. "So what?"

Mary came closer and put her hand on the cookie jar. "So it's not cookie time!" she said. "You know mom's rule. No cookies when it's close to dinner time. And that goes for your stupid friends, too."

Mary and Alex were glaring at each other. Then José started to look mad, too. "I'm not stupid, and all I'm doing is getting the cookies your brother promised me."

"Well, you can't have them. It's the rule," Mary said.

So Alex stood between two pretty big kids with the cookie jar in his hands. He didn't want to get anybody mad, but he didn't know what to do, either.

Debriefing *Questions for possible discussion:*

1 Why is it important to obey rules?

2 Who makes up the rules, anyway? Is it okay to break them if the person who made them isn't around? Why?

3 How about promises? Should you always try to keep them? Suppose you just can't keep a promise; why might that happen?

Action Period *The following pictures may be duplicated.*

Hands Off the Cookie Jar!

Alex

José

If He Hits You, Hit Him Back!

Steve

Father

If He Hits You, Hit Him Back!

Bill

Boy

Grades: 1, 3
Issues: authority, sharing

Mrs. Jeffrey's Surprise

Warm-up

(*Children's experiences*) ASK "How many of you help with jobs around the house? Are there any of you who help other people in your neighborhood? What do you do?"

OR (*Teacher's experience*) SHARE your childhood memories of things like running errands, shoveling

snow, or raking leaves for older people in your neighborhood.

THEN SAY "Our story today is about some children who help an old lady in their neighborhood."

Mrs. Jeffrey's Surprise

Mrs. Jeffrey was very old, and she had trouble doing all the work around her house. Sometimes the children in the neighborhood came over to help her. That always made Mrs. Jeffrey very happy.

One day a girl named Tina had nothing at all to do, so she decided to visit Mrs. Jeffrey and see if any work needed to be done. Mrs. Jeffrey came to the door and looked very happy to see Tina. "I really need some weeds pulled in the yard," she said. Actually, Tina didn't like pulling weeds much, but she liked to help Mrs. Jeffrey. So Tina agreed to pull weeds, and she went out to the front yard.

After she'd been pulling weeds a few minutes, her friend Sam came along. "Hi," Sam said. "Looks to me like you're doing some pretty yucky work there."

"Yucky is right," Tina said. "But Mrs. Jeffrey needs it done, so I'm doing it."

"I can't stay long," Sam said, "but I'll help you for a few minutes."

The two kids started to pull weeds together, and that made it a lot more fun. But after a little bit, they heard Sam's mother calling. "Gee," Sam said, "I've got to go now."

"Okay," Tina said, and she went back to work alone.

In just a few minutes, Mrs. Jeffrey came to

the door. "Tina," she said, "you've worked really hard today. I know that isn't a pleasant job. Come on in, and let me give you a surprise."

Tina hadn't expected this. Mrs. Jeffrey hardly ever gave anybody anything except a big smile and a thank you. But today Mrs. Jeffrey handed her a little bag and said that Tina could open it when she got home.

So Tina said thank you and skipped home with the mysterious bag. She took it into her room and closed the door. Tina then plopped down on her bed and opened the bag. In it were five delicious-looking chocolate candies.

"Oh," she said to herself, "these are really nice." Then Tina had a thought. "Maybe I should give some of them to Sam because he helped me. I wonder how many we should each get?"

Just then there was a knock at the door. It was Tina's big sister. Quickly Tina hid the candies under the bed. Tina's sister always wanted something Tina had. Sometimes she was even mean to Tina about it.

"Come on in," Tina said.

"How come you had the door closed?" her sister asked. "Are you hiding something?"

Can you help Tina quickly before her sister finds the bag?

Debriefing   *Questions for possible discussion:*

1   Is it always a good idea to share?

2   Are there times when it's better not to share?

3   Should you always do what someone bigger tells you to do?

Action Period   *The following pictures may be duplicated.*

Mrs. Jeffrey's Surprise

Tina

Sam

Mrs. Jeffrey's Surprise

Sister

Candy

The Haunted House

Grades: 1, 2, 3
Issues: authority, friendship

Warm-up

(*Children's experiences*) ASK "How many of you have lived in the same house all your life? How many of you have ever moved to a new house? How did it feel not to know anybody in the new place?"

OR (*Teacher's experience*) SHARE with the children your own early experience in moving, and describe how you felt being in a new place with no friends.

THEN SAY "Let's listen to a story about a girl who moves into a new house and has no friends at all."

The Haunted House

Dorene sometimes felt lonely. She had just moved into a new house, and school hadn't started. She really didn't have any friends yet. There were kids who lived on the block, but they were always busy doing their own things and didn't pay much attention to her. So, mostly, Dorene just played in her own yard and sometimes watched the kids go by. They were friendly enough when they did. Dorene would wave and say hi, and they would say hi back. The problem was that they just kept going.

One day, just before school was going to start, the kids went by and said hi. Only this time, one of the boys stopped and said, "Hey, you want to come with us?"

"Sure," Dorene said. "I'll have to tell my mother first."

"Okay," the boy said, "but hurry."

Dorene hurried inside and got her mother's permission to play with the kids. Then, feeling very, very happy to have some friends at last, she hurried down the street with them.

As the afternoon quickly passed, Dorene was still really happy. She liked these kids, and they really did fun things. They were just like her friends from the old neighborhood. She

was sorry that the time was going so fast. She'd have to go home and eat supper soon.

"Hey," said Lisa, one of her new friends, "let's show Dorene the haunted house."

"Yeah," agreed the others, "we can take her through it."

Dorene knew what they were talking about. A few days earlier, she was driving in the car with her mother and father and had seen the house. It was big and old and looked as though it was ready to fall over. Its windows were all broken, and its boards were coming off everywhere.

Dorene remembered what her father had said about the house. Her father had called it a wreck and said it should be torn down. He said it looked so unsafe that, if anybody went into it, they could very easily get hurt.

"Listen," her father had said, "I saw some kids playing around that house the other day. They must not know how dangerous it is. You do, and I don't want you to go near it."

But now Lisa was shouting, "Let's go."

"Wait a minute, you guys," said Dorene.

"What's wrong?" a boy asked. "Are you chicken?"

Dorene said . . .

Debriefing   *Questions for possible discussion:*

1   How do you decide that you want a person to be your friend?

2   Why is it a good idea to do what your parents tell you to do?

3   Do all parents have the same rules for their children?

4   Why do friends sometimes ask you to do things that your parents don't like?

Action Period   *The following pictures may be duplicated.*

The Haunted House

Dorene

House

The Haunted House

Lisa

Kids

Grades: 1, 2, 3
Issues: friendship, promises

**Grades: 1, 2, 3
Issues: friendship, promises**

Grandma Likes Baseball

Warm-up

(*Children's experiences*) ASK "Have the kids in your neighborhood ever made something all together? Can you tell a little bit about it?"

OR (*Teacher's experience*) SHARE with the children a time when you have made a commitment to someone and then received an attractive, but conflicting, invitation.

THEN SAY "Let's listen to a story about two brothers who were working with all the kids in the neighborhood on a special project. They found they also had a special problem."

Grandma Likes Baseball

Whenever people walked down Elm Street, they passed by the empty lot on the corner. They always stopped and took a long look at the big tree on the lot. Then they almost always said something. Sometimes they said, "That's going to be one beautiful tree house." Other times they said, "Can you believe every child in the neighborhood has helped to make that house?" It was true, too. All the children helped with the tree house when they got through with their schoolwork or whatever they had to do at home.

Peter and Matthew, who were brothers, especially liked to work on the tree house, and today was to be an important day. All the kids in the neighborhood were supposed to come to the tree house right after lunch. If everyone worked very hard, they would be through with all the building before dinner time. Everybody had promised to come.

Just when Peter and Matthew were getting ready for lunch, the phone rang. "I'll get it," yelled Peter from the kitchen. "I'll get it," yelled Matthew from the bedroom. And they both picked up extension phones at the same time. "Hello," they both said.

Then they heard their grandmother laugh. "Hi, you two! What a treat to get both of you at the same time." The boys laughed, too. They liked their grandmother a lot, and it was always special when she called or came to see

them.

"Guess what!" grandma said.

"What?" asked both boys at the same time.

"Well," she answered, "your Uncle Mike just gave me three tickets to the ball game this afternoon because they decided they couldn't go. I said I sure would like to have those tickets because I knew two boys who love ball games."

There was silence for a few moments.

"Boys?" grandma said. "Don't you want to go?"

"Sure we do," Peter answered, "only . . ."

"Only what?"

"Only . . . uh, grandma, we'd better call you back."

"Right," Matthew added, "we'd better call you back."

"Of course, dears," grandma said. "I'll be waiting to hear from you." She sounded disappointed.

The boys hung up and met each other in the kitchen.

"We promised the other kids . . ." began Peter.

At the same time, Matthew was saying, "We can't disappoint grandma. Besides, it would be fun to go to the game."

They looked at each other. "What do we do now?" they asked.

Debriefing *Questions for possible discussion:*

1 Why do people say you shouldn't let your friends down? Are there times that you have to break your promises to them even if you don't want to?

2 What does it mean to keep a promise? Are there times when you just have to break one?

Action Period *The following pictures may be duplicated.*

Grandma Likes Baseball

Peter

Matthew

Grandma Likes Baseball

Grandma

Kids

Don't Worry, We'll Be Careful!

Grades: 1, 2, 3
Issues: friendship, property, sharing

Warm-up

(*Concrete object*) SHOW the children an electronic game. ASK "How many of you know what this is? What does it do? Suppose this game were yours. Do you think you'd let other kids play with it? Why?"

OR (*Children's experiences*) ASK "How many of you have electronic games? What kind? Suppose

somebody wanted to borrow it. How would you feel?"

THEN SAY "Today's story is about an electronic game that everybody wants to play with."

Don't Worry, We'll Be Careful!

Even though Allison had toys of her own, her very favorite toy didn't belong to her at all. It was her big sister Terri's, and it was a memory game. The memory game was round, and when you turned it on, it had different colored lights on it. If you touched the lights, the game played some music. Then you had to try to make the same music yourself. One day Terri told Allison that she could play with the game for a while.

"Be careful with it," Terri said, "and you can play with it all morning if you want to. Just don't scratch it or anything."

Allison felt very happy and took the game to her room. She started trying out the music the different colors made. After a few minutes, she heard some voices outside. Allison looked out the window and saw three of her friends walking down the street.

"Hey," she yelled, "where are you going?"

"Nowhere," they answered. "Why don't you come out?"

Allison picked up the game and ran outside. "Look," she said, "Terri's letting me keep her

game all morning."

"Hey, that's really neat," one of the kids said. "Can I try it?"

"Oh, I don't think I should let you," Allison answered. She was thinking that these kids didn't take care of their toys as well as she and Terri did. Terri had told her that she should be sure that the game didn't get hurt.

"Aw, come on," one of the kids was saying. "Let us have a little turn playing with it. We'll be careful."

"Yeah," somebody else said, "we're your friends, and friends are supposed to share, aren't they?"

Allison just stood there for a minute. She was wondering what to do.

"We won't be your friends anymore if you don't let us play with it," one of the kids said.

"That's right," the other two added.

Allison wanted to keep her friends. She also knew that they might hurt the game even if they said they'd be careful, and she had promised Terri that nothing would happen to the game. She really didn't know what to do.

Debriefing   *Questions for possible discussion:*

1   Should you always share things with your friends? Is it ever okay not to share things with your friends? When?

2   Does the fact that something belongs to somebody else mean that you should treat it differently than your own things? Why?

3   If somebody wouldn't let you use something of his or hers, should you stop being that person's friend? Why?

Action Period   *The following pictures may be duplicated.*

Don't Worry, We'll Be Careful!

Allison

Terri

Don't Worry, We'll Be Careful!

Friends

Game

Grades: 2, 3
Issues: authority, promises, rules, truth

Trouble in the Tree House

Warm-up

(*Children's experiences*) ASK "Have you ever seen other kids doing things that you thought they shouldn't be doing? How did you feel about it?"

OR (*Children's experiences*) ASK "Has your brother or sister ever done something that really got you angry?"

THEN SAY "In this story, Linda sees her brother do something he shouldn't do. This causes a problem for Linda. Let's listen and see if we can help her with this problem."

Trouble in the Tree House

All the kids in the neighborhood had built a wonderful tree house. After it was finished, they all got together and decided they should make some rules. That way, nobody would get mad at anybody, and everybody could stay friends. There were about five or six rules, but the only one that matters for this story is the rule about no tattling.

The children decided that anybody who wanted to tattle about things that happened at school or at home could do it. But nobody would tattle on anybody about what happened in the tree house.

One day, not too long after this rule was made up, one of the girls (her name was Linda) decided to go over to the tree house and see if there was anybody over there to play with. When she went inside, Linda was surprised to see her brother Glenn there, and two other boys besides.

"Hi," Linda said.

The boys just looked back at her and didn't say anything. Then they started to laugh and choke a little at the same time. Linda saw that their mouths were full of something.

"Okay," she said, "what are you eating?"

One of the boys pulled out a bag of cookies.

Then another boy held up another bag. Finally, Glenn held up a third bag, and it was a big one and looked familiar.

"Hey," Linda said, "those are our cookies. Mom told us we weren't supposed to open that package until tomorrow."

Glenn just laughed some more. So did the other boys.

"I'm telling!" Linda said, and she started out of the tree house.

"No fair!" Glenn yelled. "You're not supposed to tattle about what goes on in the tree house."

"That's right," the other two boys said.

Linda felt rather angry, but she said, "Oh, okay. But you better not do it again." Then she went home. She walked in the back door, and there was her mother in the kitchen.

"Have you seen that new bag of cookies?" her mother asked. "Your Aunt Jean just came over, and I thought we could have some cookies with our coffee."

Linda felt her face turn red, and she didn't know what to say. She wanted to tell her mother the truth, of course, but she wanted to keep the rule about not tattling, too. What do you think Linda will say?

Debriefing   *Questions for possible discussion:*

1   Why is it important to obey rules? Is it ever okay not to obey a rule? When?

2   Why do we have rules, anyway? Who makes up the rules?

3   Is it important always to tell the truth? Are there some times when it wouldn't be good to tell the truth?

Action Period   *The following pictures may be duplicated.*

Trouble in the Tree House

Linda

Glenn

Trouble in the Tree House

Mother

Boys

Grades: 2, 3
Issues: friendship, rules

Tattletale, Tattletale!

Warm-up

(*Children's experiences*) ASK "Have you ever had someone tell on you when you've done something wrong? Have you ever wanted to tell on somebody, but you were afraid it was tattling?"

OR (*Teacher's experience*) SAY "When I was a child, we had a poem that went like this: 'Tattletale, tattletale, / Stick your nose in ginger ale.' Why do you think kids said this?"

THEN SAY "This is a story about a boy who had a problem with tattling."

Tattletale, Tattletale!

Alan used to be a tattletale. Finally, though, he got tired of having kids get mad at him and tired of seeing that "oh, no, here we go again" look on his teacher's face. So now he hardly ever tattled at all. The children in his class liked him better, and his teacher didn't get angry with him.

This morning Alan came to school feeling just a little nervous. He and all the other kids were going to take some tests to see how well they could read and do other things with words. Alan's teacher had said that these tests were very important and she wanted the children to do as well as they could. Alan wanted to do well, and that's why he was a little nervous.

All the children came in and sat down. The teacher gave them each two new, very sharp pencils. She had a smile on her face, but Alan could tell that today was different from other days. He heard her say, "Now, be sure you look only at your own paper, not anybody else's."

"Because that would be cheating," one of the children said.

"Yes," said the teacher, "that would be cheating."

Then she gave the signal to begin, and Alan started doing the work. The test was easier than he thought it would be, and he was one of the first children finished with the reading section. Because there was nothing else to do until the teacher said to stop, Alan watched the other kids working.

As he looked around the room, Alan noticed something funny about David, who sat at the next table. David didn't seem to be looking at his own paper. He was looking at someone else's. Alan watched him for a while, and then he was sure that David was cheating.

Alan looked at the teacher and hoped that she'd see what David was doing. But the teacher was looking somewhere else. Alan looked out the window for a minute and hoped that David would quit. But when he looked back, he saw that David was still sneaking peeks off other papers.

Alan knew that David wasn't following the rules about not cheating, and Alan thought that maybe he should tell the teacher. Then he remembered how many times he'd been called a tattletale. If he told, the kids might not want to be his friends again.

What can Alan do?

Debriefing   *Questions for possible discussion:*

1   Is it ever okay to tell on someone? When?

2   How do you decide if telling on someone is the right thing to do?

Action Period   *The following pictures may be duplicated.*

Tattletale, Tattletale!

Alan

David

Tattletale, Tattletale!

Teacher

Kids

Grades: 2, 3
Issues: authority, property

Mean Ronnie

Warm-up

(*Children's experiences*) ASK "Did you ever play with someone you didn't like very much just because there was nothing better to do? How did you feel about it?"

OR (*Children's experiences*) ASK "Have you ever been with a group of kids who did something that you didn't think was right? How did you feel about it?"

THEN SAY "Our story today is about Susan, a girl who had just the type of problem we're talking about."

Mean Ronnie

Ronnie was the biggest, meanest kid on the block. Susan was usually scared of him, too. Today, though, Ronnie came out of his house when he saw that Susan was riding around on her bike, and he had a friendly look on his face.

"Hi," he said.

Susan looked at Ronnie very carefully. She couldn't see any meanness at all. "Hi," she said back. She didn't get too close, though, just in case.

"How come you're not playing with your friends?" Ronnie asked.

"Everyone's gone today."

Ronnie said, "Me, too. All my friends are gone, too. How about if I get my bike, and we'll ride to the store? Just to look around."

Susan wasn't sure she wanted to go, but there was nothing else to do, so she told her mother she was going to the store. Meanwhile Ronnie told his mother. Then off they went. Ronnie seemed friendly enough today, but Susan was a little worried about him anyway. He was still just as big, and he might get mean at any minute.

When they got to the store, Susan said she wanted to look at the dolls, and she quickly left Ronnie behind. She was sure he wouldn't follow her there and she could be alone, but in a minute he was next to her. "Hey," he said, "let's get some candy."

"I don't have any money," Susan answered, and she began looking over a doll with brown hair and a pink dress.

"You don't need any money," Ronnie answered. "Come on, I'll show you."

Susan didn't like the way Ronnie was starting to sound. It made her feel a little bit scared. She started to look at the doll's pink dress very, very carefully.

"I said, come on," Ronnie insisted. He took Susan's hand off the doll and led her to the candy counter. "Which kind do you like best?" he asked when they got there.

"I don't want any," Susan said.

"Look, I told you I'd show you how," Ronnie said. "See, all you have to do is put this little package in your pocket when nobody is looking." Ronnie looked around and then put a package in his shirt pocket. "Now," he went on, "you wait until you get outside to eat the candy."

Susan felt very worried. "You're supposed to pay money for things, not steal them," she insisted.

Ronnie was starting to get his mean look. "I told you not to worry," he said. "Now look around to be sure nobody's watching, and get your favorite kind of candy."

Susan looked around and then up at Ronnie. He seemed very, very big all of a sudden. She looked at the candy. She didn't want to steal it. She looked back at Ronnie. He hadn't gotten any smaller.

Debriefing   *Questions for possible discussion:*

1 Why do people say that you shouldn't steal?

2 If you don't want to play with someone how can you find something better to do? Can you think of ways of telling people you don't want to play with them without hurting their feelings?

3 If people are bigger than you, does it mean that you have to do what they say?

Action Period   *The following pictures may be duplicated.*

Mean Ronnie

Susan

Ronnie

Candy

Grades: 2, 3
Issues: promises, property

Melinda's Biggest Kick

Warm-up

(*Children's experiences*) ASK "How many of your parents have ever asked you to promise that you wouldn't do something? Why did they want you to make that promise?"

OR (*Teacher's experience*) SHARE your memory of restrictions, such as not crossing busy streets or not swimming alone, that your parents gave you when

you were a child. Tell why they had these restrictions.

THEN SAY "Today's story is about a girl whose parents asked her not to do something. Her promise not to do it caused a problem. Let's listen and see if we have any ideas to help her."

Melinda's Biggest Kick

When Melinda's family bought their new house, there was just one thing that her parents worried about. Her mother was the one who worried the most. She said, "I really like this house, but I'm worried about you children and the creek out in back. If we buy the house, will you promise never, never to go in the creek unless I'm there or daddy is?"

"I promise," Melinda said right away. She liked the house and wanted the family to buy it.

"I promise," said Melinda's little brother, Sean. He was only three.

One day Melinda and Sean were playing close to the creek. Mommy and daddy had gone out, and the baby-sitter was with them. They were having a good time playing with their dad's football. He had given them special permission to use it while he was gone. They said they'd take good care of it. Now the baby-sitter was helping them throw and kick it. Melinda tried not to laugh at Sean when he kicked. He was so little that the ball hardly moved at all.

Right in the middle of one of Sean's tiny kicks, they all heard the telephone ring. The baby-sitter said, "I'll go get the phone. You two keep on playing."

"Okay," Melinda and Sean both said. The

baby-sitter ran up the hill to the house. Then Melinda said to Sean, "Sean, you can kick like a bigger boy. Here, I'll show you how." She put the ball on the ground, took a few steps back, and then ran and kicked the ball as hard as she could. The ball went sailing into the air, higher then Melinda had ever kicked it before. A big smile came across her face as she saw how high it went. Then the smile changed to a frown as Melinda watched the ball fall into the creek. She ran to the edge of the water to see where it had gone. It was stuck right between two rocks. At first Melinda thought she would wait for the baby-sitter and let her get the ball. But then the water started to push the ball away from the rocks. Melinda knew there wasn't time to get the baby-sitter before the ball would go floating down the creek. She also knew she had promised not to go in the creek, but it was really very shallow in this part. Melinda was sure she could get the ball if she jumped in right away.

She looked at Sean. He was too little to tell her what to do. She looked up the hill. The baby-sitter wasn't coming back. Then she looked at the ball; it was starting to move.

Debriefing   *Questions for possible discussion:*

1   Why do parents ask children to promise that they won't do things? Do parents expect these promises to be kept all of the time?

2   Sometimes parents ask you to promise you won't do something instead of just telling you not to do it. Why do you suppose they do that?

3   Are there any times that your parents would think it would be okay for you to break a promise you made to them? When?

Action Period   *The following pictures may be duplicated.*

Melinda's Biggest Kick

Melinda

Sean

Melinda's Biggest Kick

Baby-Sitter

Parents

The Bike Trick

Warm-up

(*Children's experiences*) ASK "How many of you have ever let your friends borrow things from you? What did you lend them?"

OR (*Children's experiences*) ASK "Have you ever seen children do tricks with their bikes that you wished you could do?"

THEN SAY "This story is about a boy whose friend asks to borrow his bike so he can try a trick with it. The boy isn't sure about lending the bike. Listen and see if you can help him out."

The Bike Trick

Bobby didn't have a dirt bike of his own. His dad said they cost too much. Bobby's big brother had one, though, and Bobby was waiting until his brother outgrew it, and then he could have the bike all to himself. Sometimes his brother let Bobby use his bike, and today was one of those days.

Bobby and his friend Simon were going to ride bikes in the woods near home. Simon had his own bike, but it was an old one, and it wasn't a dirt bike, either. The boys didn't know what they wanted to do in the woods. They thought they would just follow the trail in and see if anything interesting turned up.

Sure enough, something did. By a creek they saw some boys on their dirt bikes playing a kind of game that looked like a lot of fun. First they would go up to the top of a little hill. They they would ride as fast as they could down it into the creek. At just that place there was a flat bottom across the creek. If the boys rode their bikes really fast down the hill they could coast all the way across the creek without falling in.

"Gosh, that looks like fun!" Simon said.

"It sure does," Bobby said, "but it looks a little scary too. I don't think I want to try it."

Simon said, "I'd sure like to do it. But my bike is no good. I'd have to borrow yours, Bobby."

"Sure, okay," Bobby said. Then he thought again. "Hey, wait a minute. I don't know. This bike is my brother's, you know."

Simon looked very disappointed, and Bobby felt bad. He knew Simon really wanted to use the bike and try the trick. Simon was a good friend and Bobby liked to share things with him. But then he felt worried because he knew the bike was a special one, and it might get hurt on the rocks or rusty in the water. The bike was still his brother's, after all.

"Well," Simon asked, "are you going to let me use the bike, or not?"

Debriefing   *Questions for possible discussion:*

1   Is it ever okay to use someone's property without asking them first? Why?
2   Should your friends always expect you to lend them things?

3   Are there times when you wouldn't lend things to friends?

Action Period   *The following pictures may be duplicated.*

The Bike Trick

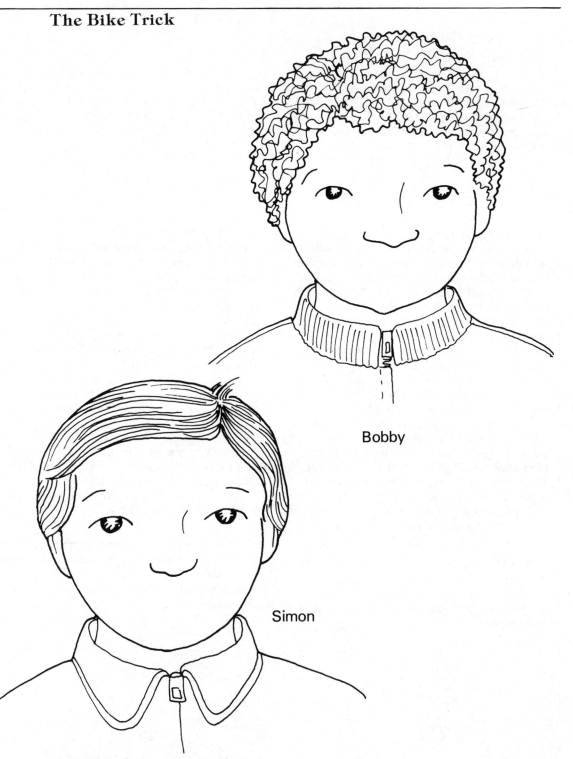

Bobby

Simon

The Bike Trick

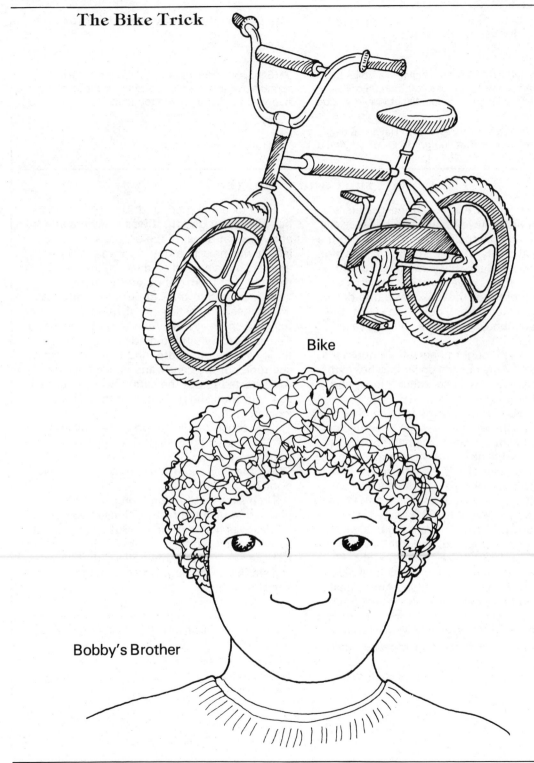

Bike

Bobby's Brother

Grades: 2, 3
Issues: friendship, sharing

The Dollar, the Candy, and the Poor Boy

Warm-up

(*Concrete object*) SHOW the children a dollar bill. ASK "What is this? Suppose you found a dollar, and it didn't belong to anyone. What would you do with it?"

OR (*Children's experiences*) ASK "Have you ever found some money that you got to keep? What did you do with it?"

THEN SAY "Today's story is about a girl who found a dollar. Let's listen and think about what happened to her after she found it."

The Dollar, the Candy, and the Poor Boy

Amy was on her way to gymnastics class. Her mom didn't have to take her, because the bus came right by their house. Amy got to the bus stop in plenty of time, so she sat down on a rock to wait. Suddenly something caught Amy's eye. It was green and it was paper, and, yes, right near the rock was a one-dollar bill. Amy looked up and down the street, but there was nobody there who could have dropped it.

"Hey," she thought to herself, "I guess it's mine now!" Amy put the dollar into her gymnastics bag along with her other things, and that's when the bus came.

After class was over, Amy felt very thirsty and hot, so she went across the street to the store, and with the dollar she had found she bought a cold drink. Amy was surprised to see that she had a lot of change left, so she decided to spend it on a bag of candy.

Then she went outside to wait for the bus to take her home. And while she waited, she started to eat the candy. Well, the bus was late, so Amy kept eating, and after a while she felt pretty stuffed. "Yuck," she thought, "I wish I hadn't eaten so much. I think I'll give the rest to Teresa." (Teresa was Amy's best friend, and they shared just about everything.)

The bus came then, and Amy picked up all her things and got on. It was really crowded, and Amy sat down in the only space that was left. It was next to a boy who was about her age. He had very old clothes on, and Amy thought that he might be pretty poor.

Amy started to think about the candy that was in her gymnastics bag. She still felt pretty full, and she really did want to give the rest to Teresa. But something made her decide, "I think I'll have one more, and that's all." So she took out the candy and chose one piece. Amy started to put the candy back in her gym bag, but then she noticed that the boy was looking at it.

"Are those candies good?" the boy asked.

"Uh, yeah," Amy said. She started to put them away again.

But the boy asked, "Are they really, really good?"

Then Amy got to wondering. She had planned to give the rest to Teresa because Teresa was her best friend. But this boy next to her looked pretty poor. Maybe he never got to have any candy. Amy noticed that he was still staring at the bag. She didn't know what she should do.

Debriefing *Questions for possible discussion:*

1 When you share, how do you know how much to give?

2 Is it all right to share different amounts with different people?

3 Suppose someone doesn't share with you. Should you share with them?

4 Do friends always share?

Action Period *The following pictures may be duplicated.*

The Dollar, the Candy, and the Poor Boy

Amy

Teresa

The Dollar, the Candy, and the Poor Boy

Poor Boy

Candy

Grades: 2, 3, 3+
Issues: friendship, promises, sharing

One More Goal To Win!

Warm-up

(*Children's experiences*) ASK "Do you have any toys you have to share with your brother or sister? How do you decide who's going to use them?"

OR (*Children's experiences*) ASK "Have you ever made a promise to someone and later wished you hadn't?"

THEN SAY "Today we're going to hear a story about a brother and sister who made a promise to each other about a toy they shared, but then they had a problem. Let's listen to see what the problem is."

One More Goal To Win!

There was only one good soccer ball in the whole neighborhood, and Mark and Jane owned it. Together. That meant they had to take turns playing with it, or they had to put all their friends together into one big game. They didn't always like doing that. Sometimes they had fights about sharing the soccer ball, and they would ask their mother what to do. She always said the same thing: "You two will just have to learn to share. I'm sure you can work this out on your own."

One Saturday morning, they both wanted to take the ball and play with their own friends. They didn't want to play together. "Okay," Mark said, "how about if I take it and play with my friends for exactly one hour? Then you take the ball and play with your friends for exactly one hour. That way nobody will get in a fight, right?"

"Why can't I get it first?" Jane asked.

"Because I got it out of the closet first," Mark answered.

"Promise you'll give it up when it's time?" Jane said.

"Promise," Mark said.

So off he went with the ball to play with his friends. They took it down to the field at the end of the block. When they got there they saw that some other boys from the next block over were already there. "Hey," Mark said, "let's challenge them to a game." Everyone agreed, and the boys decided that the first team to get four goals would be the winner.

The game was really exciting. Everyone played hard, but for the longest time the score

remained tied at three to three. Then Mark's team got the ball, and it looked as though they were very close to scoring a goal. Just then, Mark saw something out of the corner of his eye. It was his sister, Jane, coming down the street with a bunch of her girlfriends.

"Oh, no," he thought, "we've got to make this goal, quick."

But they didn't. Jane walked up right next to where they were playing and called, "Our turn. You promised."

"Come on," Mark said. "We've got to make just one more goal. It's only a few minutes more."

Jane looked mad. "You promised!" she yelled.

"Yeah," yelled all her friends, "you promised!"

One of the boys said, "Don't listen to her, Mark. This game's more important than some stupid promise." He took off with the ball, and the boys started the next play.

Just then Jane and her friends came running into the game and made it stop. "You promised, you promised," Jane was yelling.

"Come on, Mark, get your sister out of here," the boys started to yell.

Mark didn't know what to do. He always kept his promises to Jane, but if he gave the ball away, he was certain his friends wouldn't be too happy with him. Besides, he really wanted to finish the game.

Everyone seemed to be mad now. Mark didn't know what to do.

Debriefing   *Questions for possible discussion:*

1   What does it mean to make a promise?

2   Is it ever okay not to keep a promise? How would you decide if it is okay?

3   Is it more important to share things with your brothers and sisters or with your friends? Why?

Action Period   *The following pictures may be duplicated.*

One More Goal To Win!

Mark

Jane

One More Goal To Win!

Boys

Girls

Grades: 3, 3+
Issues: authority, truth

Whose Money Is It, Anyway?

Warm-up

(*Children's experiences*) ASK ''Have you ever gone door to door, selling things or collecting money? It's hard work, isn't it?''

OR (*Teacher's experience*) SHARE an experience you had as a child, selling things or collecting money.

THEN SAY ''Beverly was a good door-to-door salesperson. Here's her story.''

Whose Money Is It, Anyway?

Beverly felt very pleased with herself. Last month she had walked all over the neighborhood asking people if they would like to order some Girl Scout cookies, and she had gotten more orders than any of the other Brownies she knew.

Now Beverly had to deliver all the boxes that had just come in. With all of the orders, that was going to be a big job. She didn't mind, though, because the money from the cookie sale would help her Brownie troop. She packed the boxes into a big shopping bag and started out.

She had been delivering cookies for quite a while when she came to Mr. Johnson's house. He was a very nice man who said he just loved Girl Scout cookies, and so he had ordered three boxes. Beverly rang the bell, and there was Mr. Johnson, smiling.

''Hi,'' he said. ''Those look wonderful. Here's a five-dollar bill.''

''Well,'' Beverly said, ''that means I owe you fifty cents in change.'' She looked inside her change purse and discovered that all the change had been given out. ''I'm sorry,'' Beverly said. ''Could I bring you the change tomorrow?''

''Oh, that's okay,'' Mr. Johnson answered.

''Why don't you just keep it?''

''Hey, thanks!'' Beverly said. She really had been working pretty hard, and she was happy to have a little money all her own.

When Beverly got home and told her mother that Mr. Johnson had given her the extra money, Beverly's mother was not pleased at all. ''This isn't a time when you're earning money for yourself,'' she said. ''This is a time to help out your Brownie troop.''

''But he said I should keep it,'' Beverly argued.

''And I say you should give it back,'' her mother replied, and she sent Beverly back to Mr. Johnson's. When Beverly got there, however, there was nobody home.

Beverly thought for a minute. She supposed she should come back another time and try again, and then she would be obeying her mother. But that didn't seem fair to her. Mr. Johnson had given her the money, and it had been his money, not her mother's. She felt a little angry at her mother, but she knew she should obey, too. Beverly didn't want to go home until she had made up her mind. She was pretty sure her mother wouldn't think to ask if Mr. Johnson had been home or not. So Beverly could do anything she wanted . . .

Debriefing *Questions for possible discussion:*

1 What do you do if someone bigger than you tells you to do something that you don't think is fair?

2 Why do people say it's important to tell the truth?

3 If someone doesn't ask you for the truth, do you still have to tell it?

Action Period *The following pictures may be duplicated.*

Whose Money Is It, Anyway?

Beverly

Mother

Mr. Johnson

Fifty Cents

Grades: 3, 3+
Issues: promises, property, truth

Just Don't Bug Me Anymore!

Warm-up

(*Children's experiences*) SAY "Did you ever see a really good friend do something wrong, and you didn't know what to do about it? How did you feel, trying to decide what to do?"

OR (*Teacher's experience*) SHARE with the children a time when you had a tough decision to make

about telling on a friend. Emphasize the difficulty of deciding rather than the outcome.

THEN SAY "There's a girl in today's story that had just such a problem. It wasn't a very happy time for her. Maybe you can help out."

Just Don't Bug Me Anymore!

The going-home bell was just about to ring, and Kathy was feeling restless. Mr. Rogers, the teacher, said he had an important announcement to make, but Kathy just wanted to go home. So she was only half listening when Mr. Rogers said, "Now, I know that envelope with the book club orders and money in it was right in this drawer. I've spent three days looking everywhere for it, and now I guess I need your help. Someone must have taken it." Kathy stared out the window, not really listening, until suddenly she had a horrible thought. Instead of seeing the trees outside, she was seeing a picture in her mind that told her what might have happened to the money.

Three days before, just after lunch, Kathy had come into the room and nobody was there except her best friend, Beth. Beth had been standing near Mr. Rogers's desk and she'd had a funny look on her face. Then Kathy remembered something else. For the last three days Beth had been treating her friends to candy bars after school. Kathy had wondered where Beth's extra money had come from, and now she was afraid she knew.

While Mr. Rogers talked, Kathy tried not to look at Beth, but she couldn't help herself. Beth's face looked extra red, and she was staring at the floor. Usually Kathy and Beth walked home together, but today Kathy just wanted to be alone. She hurried out the door, but about a block later she heard Beth calling to her, so she decided she'd better wait.

Breathlessly, Beth announced, "Kathy,

you're my best friend so I just have to tell you something I did." And then she said she'd taken the money, and she wished she hadn't.

"Well, give it back, then," Kathy said. She was feeling a little angry.

"I can't," Beth answered. "I've already spent most of it. I wouldn't ever do it again, you know. Hey, I know what! I can pay you back your part, Kathy."

Kathy felt a little better at first, but then she said, "Well, it's still not fair to the other kids. None of them will be able to get the books they ordered now."

"I guess I really made a mistake, didn't I?" Beth said. "You won't tell, will you? I promise I'll never do anything like that again."

"Oh, all right," Kathy answered. "Just don't bug me anymore, okay?" And she hurried home without looking back at Beth.

After a couple of days, Mr. Rogers called Kathy to his desk. "Kathy," he said, "I've been noticing that you and Beth aren't very good friends lately. In fact, you seem to be acting very badly toward her. Would you like to talk about it?"

"It's nothing," Kathy said. "Just nothing at all."

Mr. Rogers looked at her hard. "Yes, Kathy," he said, "it's something. I think you'd better tell me about it, don't you?"

Kathy thought about the promise she'd made to Beth, and then she thought about all the kids who had lost their book money. Mr. Rogers was waiting for her answer.

Debriefing   *Questions for possible discussion:*

1   Why is it important to keep a promise? Are there ever times when it's a better idea to break one?

2   Why do people say you shouldn't steal? What does it mean to respect other people's property?

Why is that important?

3   What about telling the truth? What will happen if you don't? Does it matter? Why?

Action Period   *The following pictures may be duplicated.*

Just Don't Bug Me Anymore!

Kathy

Beth

Mr. Rogers

Grades: 3, 3+
Issues: property, truth

Mrs. Crabby

Warm-up

(*Children's experiences*) ASK "How many of you like to play hide-and-seek? What do you like best about the game?"

OR (*Children's experiences*) ASK "Have you ever accidentally broken something as you were playing a game? How did you feel when it happened?"

THEN SAY "Edwin and Chris really liked to play hide-and-seek. When they were playing, they ran into a problem. Let's see if we can help them with it."

Mrs. Crabby

It was a beautiful Saturday morning. Edwin and Chris rushed outside to meet all their friends. They had gotten up a big group to play hide-and-seek, so it seemed it was really going to be a fun morning.

Their neighborhood was perfect for hide-and-seek. All the yards had lots of big bushes between them, and these gave the kids plenty of places to hide. There was just one problem, though. With so many bushes, it was hard to tell exactly whose yard you were in.

That wouldn't be a problem, either, if it weren't for Mrs. Allman. She spent a lot of time working in her yard to make it beautiful and didn't like kids running through it. Because she was always scolding the kids if they went into her yard, they called her Mrs. Crabby.

The game hadn't been going on for long when Chris and Edwin found themselves looking for a hiding place together. They were running between yards so fast that they knocked over a couple of plants that were in big pots and broke a large branch partway off of a very pretty bush.

"Uh-oh," Chris said, as he lifted one of the pots upright, "these are Mrs. Crabby's plants. Now we're going to be in trouble."

"Don't worry about it," Edwin replied. "She's not home now. We can come back later and saw the branch the rest of the way off. It will still look good."

"We'll have to put more dirt in these pots, too," Chris said. "I guess they'll look okay, though."

Because they were talking about the plants,

they forgot that they were supposed to be hiding, and the girl who was it caught them right away. She got Edwin first, so he was it next.

Of course, with Edwin it, they couldn't go and get the saw right away. Then they got so wrapped up in the game that they forgot about the plants. In fact, they forgot about everything that had happened.

But then something reminded them. Once again Chris and Edwin were together looking for a hiding place, and they ran in the same direction. Suddenly, they had to stop. Someone stepped out of the bushes and stood right in front of them. It was Mrs. Crabby.

Edwin looked at Chris, and Chris looked at Edwin. They were both glad that they weren't alone.

Mrs. Crabby folded her arms and scowled. "You two know that I don't want any children running on my property."

"We didn't mean to," Edwin said. "We just weren't watching, I guess."

"Well, see that it doesn't happen again," she said. Then she pointed to the broken branch.

"Now, which children in this wild bunch out here today wrecked my plants and broke this branch?"

Again, Edwin and Chris looked at each other. They knew that they should tell the truth, but then Mrs. Crabby might tell their mother, and they would be in trouble. Besides, they were planning to fix the plants up again, anyhow.

"Well?" Mrs. Crabby asked impatiently.

Debriefing *Questions for possible discussion:*

1   Is it ever okay not to tell the truth to somebody that you don't like? When?

2   Is there any difference between breaking something on purpose and breaking it accidentally? Which is worse?

3   Is it okay to break something that belongs to someone else if they break something that belongs to you? Why?

Action Period   *The following pictures may be duplicated.*

Mrs. Crabby

Edwin

Chris

Mrs. Crabby

Mrs. Crabby

Mother

Grades: 3, 3+
Issues: authority, friendship, promises

Warm-up

(*Children's experiences*) ASK "How many of you have ever played sports on a real team? How did you decide what sport you were going to play?"

OR (*Children's experiences*) ASK "Did you ever plan to do something with your friends, and then

Max's Mess

you found out that your parents had other plans for you? What happened?"

THEN SAY "Here's a story about a boy who decided to play for a team, but whose father had other ideas."

Max's Mess

Last fall, Max played soccer for the first time. He was on a really good team, and they won most of their games. All the kids on the team wore red shirts and black shorts, and most of them were really good friends with Max.

During the winter there wasn't any soccer, but now it was spring and soccer was beginning for another season. The team had just had its first practice, and Max was really excited. Now he could play even better than he did in the fall. Maybe that's because he'd grown so much that his mom had to get him a new and bigger red shirt.

Just today, though, a problem came into Max's life when his dad came home. You see, Max's dad had never played soccer before, and he didn't like it very much. But his dad played baseball very well, and he kept trying to get Max to play it with him. Max didn't know if he liked baseball or not, because he'd never really played it. He did know he liked soccer, and he had a lot of good friends on the team.

Max didn't know that he was going to have a problem when his father said, "Hey Max! Have I ever got a surprise for you."

Max was interested right away, as you can

imagine. "Well," he said, "what is it?"

"Sit down," his dad said, "and we'll talk about it." So they sat down in the living room, and his dad continued. "Just today, Mr. Ely called me—you know Mr. Ely, don't you?"

"Sure," Max said. "That's Cal's father."

"Right. Well, anyway, Mr. Ely was looking for somebody to coach one of the baseball teams, and he asked me to do it. I said that I'd be glad to. What do you think of that, Max?"

Max thought it was great and said so. He wondered though why his dad kept looking at him so funny. Can you guess why?

Right. His dad wanted Max to quit soccer and play baseball on his team instead. "It would be a really nice thing for me to have my own son on my baseball team" was the way he said it.

"But soccer's already started," Max said, "and all my friends are on the team."

"Not Cal," his dad said. "Cal will be playing baseball. And it sure would make me happy."

"What a mess," Max thought. "I really want to play soccer, and I don't want to let my team down. But I shouldn't let my dad down, either. What'll I do now?"

Debriefing *Questions for possible discussion:*

1 If you've made a promise to a friend, and then one of your parents asks you if you want to do something else, how do you decide what to do?

2 What do you do when your parents say that you can decide something for yourself, and you really

want to decide for yourself, but you know what they want you to choose?

3 Is it always important to keep a promise? Are there ever times when you shouldn't?

Action Period *The following pictures may be duplicated.*

Max's Mess

Father

Max

Soccer Friends

Grades: 3, 3+
Issues: authority, friendship, promises

Warm-up

(*Children's experiences*) ASK "How many of you have ever been given a special job to do by your parents? How did you feel when they asked you to do that special job?"

OR (*Children's experiences*) ASK "Have you ever been at home alone and wished that you could have friends visit, but your parents said they couldn't? How did you feel?"

Abby's First Job

THEN SAY "In today's story, a girl is asked to do a special job by her mother, but she had to do this job all by herself. This causes a problem for her. Let's listen and see if we can think of some ways to deal with this problem."

Abby's First Job

Abby was feeling very important. Her mother had just asked her to baby-sit for the very first time. Of course, Abby wasn't old enough to do real baby-sitting, but this would be with Abby's baby brother. Her mother was going to visit a sick friend, and Abby would take care of the baby while he had a nap.

Mother gave Abby the phone number where she'd be. Then she told Abby not to let anybody into the house. Abby promised to do what her mother said. To tell the truth, she was feeling kind of excited about baby-sitting.

Her mom gave Abby a hug and then drove off. Abby went into the baby's room and checked on him. He was sound asleep. Then she went into the living room to read. It was very, very quiet. Pretty soon, Abby heard some funny noises out in the kitchen. She went, but there was nothing there. Then she heard noises in her bedroom. There was nothing there, either.

"I guess I'm just a little scared about being alone," she said to herself. "I'll just sit here and read and try not to worry." Abby looked at the clock. "I wish I knew when mom was going to be home," she thought. She was really beginning to feel scared.

Just then the doorbell rang. It was Abby's best friend, Kristi. "Hi," Kristi said. "Want to play?"

"I can't," Abby replied. "I'm baby-sitting."

"Wow!" said Kristi. "I wish I could do that."

"I don't know if I like it or not," Abby answered. "It's a little scary being here alone."

Kristi smiled a big, friendly smile. "Well, I'll just come in," she said, "and keep you company."

For just a second, Abby thought about what a good idea that was. Then she remembered. "Oh, I can't have anybody in. Mom said so."

Kristi looked as though her feelings had been hurt. "I'm just trying to be a good friend and help you. I'll bet your mom wouldn't even know," she said. "If you don't want me to help you, I guess we're not very good friends after all, are we?" Kristi started to leave.

Abby didn't know what to do. She sure didn't want to lose Kristi's friendship. But she didn't want to get in trouble with her mom, either. Do you have any ideas?

Debriefing   *Questions for possible discussion:*

1 Why do parents tell you not to do things? Do parents need reasons when they tell you not to do things? Why?

2 Are there some times when it is worse to disobey your parents than other times? When?

3 What are some reasons why people stop being friends? Are these good reasons? Why?

Action Period   *The following pictures may be duplicated.*

Abby's First Job

Abby

Kristi

Abby's Mother

Grades: 3, 3+
Issues: authority, friendship

Warm-up

(*Children's experiences*) ASK "How many of you like to ride horses? How many of you wish you could ride a horse?"

OR (*Children's experiences*) ASK "Did your parents ever give you a wonderful surprise for your birthday that you didn't expect? What was it?"

Stephanie and Star

THEN SAY "Here's a story about a girl who wished that she had a horse to ride. On her birthday she got an unexpected present."

Stephanie and Star

Stephanie had always wanted to own a horse. She loved horses. But she knew she'd never have one of her own.

"Too expensive," her mother said.

"Out of the question," her father agreed.

But her parents knew that Stephanie loved horses, so for her birthday they gave her a special present. It was a set of ten horseback-riding lessons. Stephanie felt really happy when her mother took her to the stables for the first lesson. She felt even happier when the teacher let her pick the horse she wanted to ride.

Stephanie chose a large, brown, friendly horse with a white star just above his nose. His name, of course, was Star. "I know just how I'm going to ride him," Stephanie thought to herself. "I'll be real gentle and just talk to him. We'll be really good friends, and he'll do just what he should."

But when Stephanie got on the horse, she had a hard time getting him to do anything. The more she talked to the horse, the more he just stood still. The teacher was on her own horse, and she just watched Stephanie for a while. Then she laughed and said, "The only way you'll get that horse to go is if you crack down on him." Then she gave Stephanie a little whip.

Stephanie felt terrible. She didn't want to hurt the horse. She wanted to be gentle with him. "Come on," the teacher was saying, "let's go. We can't sit here all day." Then the teacher leaned over and gave Stephanie's horse a whack. The horse started off immediately.

It went like that for quite a while. First Stephanie would try to get Star to go by being gentle. Then the teacher would tell Stephanie to crack down, but Stephanie would just sit there, because she didn't want to hurt the horse.

"Look," the teacher finally said, sounding exasperated, "when we started the lessons, I told you that you'd have to do what I said. Now, either you crack down on this horse, or forget the lessons."

Stephanie didn't know what to do. She wanted to be a good student, but she didn't want to hurt Star. What could she do?

Debriefing *Questions for possible discussion:*

1 Why can a teacher tell you what to do? Are there times when a teacher can't tell you what to do?

2 Why do people say that you should be kind to animals? What does being kind to animals mean?

3 Are there times when it's better not to be kind to an animal?

Action Period *The following pictures may be duplicated.*

Stephanie and Star

Teacher

Stephanie

Stephanie's Parents

Last One In Is a Rotten Fried Egg!

Grades: 3, 3+
Issues: friendship, rules

Warm-up

(*Children's experiences*) ASK "How many of you can swim? Are there lifeguards where you go swimming? Why are they there?"

OR (*Children's experiences*) ASK "Do any of your moms and dads have safety rules for you to follow? Do you always remember them?"

THEN SAY "Grown-ups make lots of rules to keep children safe, don't they? Here's a story about a girl who wondered if she should break one of those rules."

Last One In Is a Rotten Fried Egg!

It was a really hot summer's day. Do you know how hot it was? It was so hot that the kids on Cindy's block were thinking they ought to try to fry an egg on the sidewalk. But nobody's mother would give them an egg, so they decided to think up something else.

"How about a swim in the river?" somebody asked.

"Again?" the other kids said. "We did that this morning."

"Well," Cindy said, "can anybody think of anything any cooler?"

Nobody could, so all the kids (there were eight or nine of them) decided to go back down to the river for a swim. They all went home for their bathing suits and to check with their mothers.

Now, all the mothers in the block had the same rule: no swimming in the river unless the lifeguard was on duty. That never seemed to be a problem, though, because the lifeguard was always there.

Cindy and all the others met at the top of the hill that led down to the water. All their mothers had said it was okay to go, so everybody was happy. Soon they would be cool, too. Down the hill they all raced and decided that the last one in the water would be a rotten egg.

"No," laughed Cindy. "The last one will be a rotten *fried* egg." Everybody else laughed, too, and down they went. At the water's edge, they all stopped suddenly. Not one child jumped in. Do you know why?

It was because the lifeguard wasn't sitting in the lifeguard chair. The children looked all around them, but he was nowhere to be seen.

Cindy went over to a lady sitting on a blanket and asked, "Do you know where the lifeguard is?"

"Yes, I do," the lady answered. "He wasn't feeling well, so he went home."

"Oh, rats," some of the kids said.

"Now we'll have to leave," said some others.

Then Mike, the biggest boy, said, "Hey, I have an idea. We're all good swimmers, aren't we?"

"Sure," everybody said.

"Why don't we swim and just be careful?" Mike suggested.

Everyone looked very uncertain. Finally, somebody said, "Maybe we could just wade."

All of them thought that was a great idea, and they decided that it would be okay if they just went in up to their knees. They decided it really wasn't swimming.

All except Cindy. "I think when our mothers made up the no-swimming rule, they meant not getting in the water at all," she said. "You do what you want, but I'm going home."

Everybody looked uncertain again, except for Mike. "Baby!" he said, "You're nothing but a baby."

"Yeah," all the others said then, "you're nothing but a baby."

"Nothing's going to happen," said Mike. "We're just going to wade, that's all. Come on, Cindy."

"Yeah, Cindy," everybody said.

Cindy felt unhappy inside, even though she tried to smile at the kids. She wanted to be a friend, but she wanted to follow the rules, too. What do you think she could do?

Debriefing *Questions for possible discussion:*

1 Are safety rules more important to keep than other kinds of rules? Why?

2 How do you know when somebody else is really your friend? What is a friend, anyway?

Action Period *The following pictures may be duplicated.*

Last One In Is a Rotten Fried Egg!

Mike

Cindy

Children

Grades: 3, 3+
Issues: rules, sharing

The Ice Cream Special

Warm-up

(*Children's experiences*) ASK "How many of you like ice cream? Suppose I told you that you could have any kind of ice cream sundae that you wanted. What kind would you have?"

OR (*Children's experiences*) ASK "Did you ever have to decide between two things and wish that you could have both?"

THEN SAY "Today's story is about two children who had to choose between two kinds of ice cream treats."

The Ice Cream Special

Once a month, the ice cream store at the mall had a special sale just for kids under twelve. For ten cents you could have an ice cream cone, and for fifty cents you could make your own sundae. Leslie liked that. Even though her mother thought she shouldn't have a lot of sweets, she always let her make the sundae as a special treat. And, boy, did she put on the toppings! Hot fudge, marshmallow, strawberries, butterscotch, cherries—she could hardly taste the ice cream when she was finished. Since you could have as many toppings as you wanted, she sometimes went back for seconds.

Every month on the ice cream day, Leslie and her friend Don would go to the mall with one of their mothers. First they'd shop a little with her, and then she'd drop them off at the ice cream store and do some more shopping while the children made their sundaes and ate them.

Today was ice cream day. When they were shopping, though, Don found a toy space monster that he really liked. As he was paying for it, he told Leslie, "Oh, well, I guess I can't have a sundae today. I can only have an ice

cream cone. I just have ten cents left. But that's okay. I really wanted this space monster, so I don't care."

Don changed his mind when they got to the ice cream store, though. When he saw the sundaes that other kids had made, his mouth watered. They certainly looked a lot nicer than the tiny cone he was going to have to buy.

Don sat down at a table with his cone and waited for Leslie to finish making her sundae. When she came over with it, Don looked at it carefully. Leslie had put on strawberries, whipped cream, and pineapple. It looked a lot better than his cone.

"Hey," Don whispered to Leslie. "Why don't I push my ice cream down into the cone so there's some room on top. Then you could put some of your strawberries and stuff on it." Don saw that Leslie was looking at him funny, so he said, "It's okay. You can go back and put some more on yours."

"I don't think I should," Leslie said.

"Hey, come on and be a friend," Don said. "Nobody's looking now."

Leslie looked around. It was true. Nobody was looking. Still, she didn't know . . .

Debriefing *Questions for possible discussion:*

1 Is it ever okay to do something that's against the rules as long as no one's looking?

2 Are there ever times when it's better not to share?

Action Period *The following pictures may be duplicated.*

The Ice Cream Special

Don

Leslie

Sundae

Cone

Who Takes the Cake?

Grades: 3, 3+
Issues: promises, sharing

Warm-up

(*Children's experiences*) ASK "How many of you have ever cooked something with a friend? What did you make? How did it taste?"

OR (*Children's experiences*) ASK "How many of you have ever forgotten your lunch? What did you do for food?"

THEN SAY "Here's a story about two girls who cooked something together and a boy who forgot his lunch."

Who Takes the Cake?

Barbara was singing as she packed her lunch for the bike ride and picnic. She just knew she was going to have a good time with her friends. First she made herself a peanut butter and honey sandwich. That was her favorite kind. Then she washed and dried a very red apple and put it into the bag along with the sandwich. Finally, Barbara cut two big pieces of chocolate cake and packed them in also. She wasn't planning to eat both those pieces of cake. One was for her friend Ginny, who was going on the bike ride, too. Ginny had helped Barbara and her mom bake the cake last night. Barbara had promised Ginny that she'd put an extra piece of cake in for her.

Barbara put her lunch and some orange juice in her backpack, got on her bike, and headed down to Ginny's house. "Have you got the cake?" Ginny asked.

"Of course I do," Barbara answered. "I promised, didn't I?"

Next they went by Jeff's house to pick him up, and finally all three of them stopped by Doug's. There were four of them, Barbara, Ginny, Jeff, and Doug, riding their bikes to the park on the other side of town. When they got there, the kids decided they weren't hungry yet, so they played on the swings and slides for a while. Then they played a couple of games, and by that time they were all hungry and thirsty.

The four kids sat under a big oak tree and opened their packs. For a minute, it was very quiet while everyone got out food.

Then Doug said, "Oh, no! I can't believe I did it!"

"Did what?" the others said, all together.

"Forgot my lunch," Doug groaned.

"Hey, that's okay," Jeff said. "I brought an extra half sandwich just in case I was real hungry. You can have that."

"Gee, thanks," Doug said.

Ginny reached in her bag. "I brought a whole bunch of raisins," she said. "I don't need them all."

Barbara looked in her bag. You know what she had, don't you? Just a sandwich and an apple and, yes, two pieces of cake. She knew she'd promised one piece to Ginny, but here was Doug without any lunch. She figured Ginny wouldn't mind.

"Well, Doug," Barbara said. "I have two pieces of cake. I guess you could have one if Ginny doesn't mind."

Ginny looked at her. "Hey, you promised!" she said. Barbara could see that she was getting angry. "I helped make that cake, and you promised. You already have enough to eat, don't you, Doug?"

Doug looked kind of embarrassed. "Well, not really," he said.

Barbara didn't know what to do next. Doug was hungry and wanted the cake. But she'd promised Ginny, hadn't she? Can you help her decide?

Debriefing   *Questions for possible discussion:*

1   Why do people keep promises? Are there ever times when it's okay not to keep a promise?

2   Is it important to share? Why?

3   How do you know how much to share?

4   Should friends always expect you to share? Are there times when you wouldn't share with friends?

Action Period   *The following pictures may be duplicated.*

Who Takes the Cake?

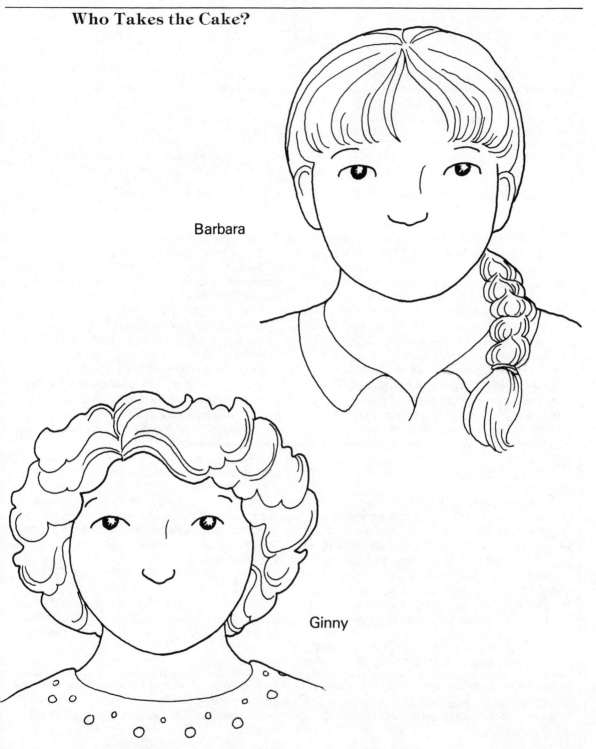

Barbara

Ginny

Who Takes the Cake?

Doug

Jeff

Cake

Grades: 3, 3+
Issues: friendship, promises

Adrian's Sunday

Warm-up

(*Children's experiences*) ASK "How many of you have ever been really bored on a Saturday or Sunday afternoon? What did you do?"

OR (*Children's experiences*) ASK "Have you ever wanted to keep a promise, but then something that seemed just as important came up?"

THEN SAY "Today we're going to hear a story about a girl who had just such a problem. I want you to listen carefully to see how she can solve her problem."

Adrian's Sunday

It was another dull Sunday afternoon. Adrian was really bored. This Sunday was worse than others because Lynn, Adrian's best friend, was at her grandmother's house for the weekend. At least when Lynn was here, they could find something to do. Today, however, just dragged and dragged. As she was trying for what felt like the hundredth time to think of something to do, the phone rang.

"Hi, Adrian, this is Stacy. What are you doing?"

"Nothing."

"Well, why don't you come over to my house? My parents are going to visit some people, and I don't want to go with them. They said I could stay home if one of my friends came over and kept me company. Do you want to come? We can play records on the stereo."

Adrian was surprised. She hadn't been particularly friendly with Stacy. In fact, she and Lynn seldom said anything more than hi to her. Stacy was okay, but Adrian and Lynn had a good time just hanging around with each other.

Adrian paused a moment. "Well, okay," she said. There really wasn't anything else to do anyway.

"Good. I'm so glad I don't have to go with them. It's so boring. Here, tell my mother that you'll come. She said I couldn't stay home alone."

After Adrian told Stacy's mother that she would come over, Adrian gathered some records to take with her.

Just as she started to leave, the phone rang again.

"Adrian," an excited voice on the phone said, "it's Lynn. We came home early. You've got to come right over and see the things my grandmother gave me."

"What did you get?" Adrian asked.

"Oh, lots of really neat things. When are you coming?"

"Well," Adrian said . . .

Debriefing   *Questions for possible discussion:*

1   Is it ever okay to break a promise? When would it be right?

2   Why do we usually try to keep our promises?

3   Is it more important to avoid hurting your best friend's feelings than anyone else's?

4   Why does it matter if you hurt someone's feelings, anyway?

Action Period   *The following pictures may be duplicated.*

Adrian's Sunday

Lynn

Adrian

Stacy

CHAPTER

5

Making Your Own

Taking Up Where We Leave Off

Children have distinct personalities, characters, backgrounds, and experiences; together, your students form a group different from any with which you have worked or will work. Each group has its own personality, interests, needs, and ways of interacting.

We had to base the decision stories in this book on experiences common to the lives of all children. We tested these stories, and they worked with various groups; they undoubtedly will work with your group, too. But we encourage you to try your hand at developing decision stories that especially suit your students.

It is not difficult. All you need to keep in mind is the characteristics of a decision story and the strategies for putting one together.

Characteristics of a Decision Story

First, a decision story is relevant to the children for whom it is prepared, so that they can grasp it easily; the story presents a problem that they could encounter themselves in real life. To determine whether a story is indeed within the sphere of experience of your students, ask yourself the following questions. Is the problem one that the children could face in their own lives? Is the story believable? Will the story hold the children's interest? The answer to each question must be yes.

Second, a decision story contains a conflict between values that the children hold as roughly equal in importance. As we say in chapter one, the children with whom we have worked seem to value seven social goods above all others: telling the truth, obeying people in authority, obeying rules, respecting other people's property, sharing, keeping promises, and honoring friendship. (Other issues may be as important to specific groups of children.)

These seven values, however, vary in importance among children of various ages. We have learned from our research that children at different grade levels perceive some issues as much more important then others. If a decision story pits one value against another, and the children see one as much more important, the story presents no dilemma, as far as the children are concerned. Suppose, for example, you write a story presenting a conflict between telling the truth and friendship. If your children perceive telling the truth to be much more important than friendship (as many second and third graders actually do), they will more or less automatically decide in favor of the former; they will see no real contest, and the decision story session will teach them little.

In the interviews we conducted with almost 200 children, we found general agreement at each grade level concerning which social goods would or would not conflict in decision making. The following chart illustrates, by grade, those that conflict so little in children's opinions that, generally speaking, there would be no point in creating a story in which they are central to the plot. The pairs are listed so that the more highly valued is first.

No-Contest Pairs

kindergarten	none
first grade	(1) rules/friendship, (2) rules/sharing
second grade	(1) truth/sharing, (2) truth/friendship, (3) truth/property, (4) rules/sharing, (5) rules/friendship, (6) authority/sharing
third grade	truth/friendship
fourth grade	(1) truth/sharing, (2) truth/property, (3) rules/sharing, (4) rules/property
fifth grade	(1) truth/sharing, (2) truth/property, (3) rules/sharing

Third, a decision story is open-ended. The dilemma that the story presents is not resolved within the story, nor is the resolution predictable on the basis of the story. In fact, a decision story should have more than two potential resolutions, because most decisions the children face in life do not involve simple either/or questions. And each potential resolution must be plausible; the story must not be loaded so that only one or two endings are credible.

Two Strategies for Composing Decision Stories

To write a decision story, either you can choose an issue you want the children to address and then construct a plot that presents it, or you can invent a story and then determine if a conflict of values does, or could, occur within it.

Choosing the Issue First

If you decide to choose the issue before composing the story, then follow these six steps:

1 *Choose two or more values that can conflict in your students' lives,* by thinking about problems your students have experienced and their possible underlying causes, or by referring to our discussion of conflicting and nonconflicting values above.

2 *Imagine concrete situations in which these values could conflict for your students.* Look again to the everyday lives and problems of your students. You can also look to your own childhood experiences for inspiration. (Problems seem to recur; your students face many of the dilemmas you faced as a child.)

3 *Construct a rough plot* based on one of the situations you imagined in step two. Sketch out the situation, how the problem develops, and how the problem surfaces.

4 *Make sure the problem is open to more than two resolutions.* The situation should not present a simple either/or choice. Imagine as many possible endings as you can. If you cannot think of more than two, your students probably will not be able to, either.

5 *Flesh out the story,* giving it body and life. Make certain that the story takes place at a specific time and location and has characters that are believable. Make the story as interesting as possible to the children.

6 *Make sure the story does not point to one specific ending.* In step four, you determined that there are several possible resolutions. Now make certain that you have written the story to allow the

children to suggest most, if not all, of them. First, one resolution must not flow as if inexorably from the story's last words. (If a story contains a conflict between doing what a child's friend wants and doing what the child's mother, an authority figure, wants, for example, place the mother elsewhere when the child must weigh options; the mother's presence would tip the scales.) Second, make sure that all possible resolutions are more or less equally attractive to the children. And try not to present one possible resolution early and another much later in the story.

Writing the Story First

If you decide to compose a story and then see if values do, or could, conflict in it, follow these steps:

1   *Outline a story that presents a problem that could arise in your students' lives.* You can reflect, for inspiration, on dilemmas you faced as a child or that you have seen your students face. Outline what happened to cause a certain problem to develop and how the problem presented itself.

2   *See if this problem contains, or could contain, an issue involving values of roughly equal weight.* Ask yourself if the main character is required to choose among two or more values, such as obeying authority and telling the truth. If so, then proceed to develop the story more fully. If not, ask yourself if there is any way to introduce such a conflict. Be careful not to force issues into a story, however; if the plot is artificial, your students will not be interested in it.

3   *Proceed as you would in steps four, five, and six, "Choosing the Issue First," above.* Make sure the problem in your story does not involve a no-contest issue for your students' grade level (see chart, page 136). Make sure the story's problem is open to more than two resolutions; flesh out the story; and, finally, make sure the story does not point to one specific ending.

Hints for Making and Using Decision Stories

If you choose to look for inspiration to your students' experiences, you may reflect on problems that have occurred in the classroom, on the playground, and in other places that you have seen children interact. Do not base your plot in detail on any of the actual problems you observe, however; the story would be too threatening. Instead, look for the conflicts underlying the actual situations, and work these conflicts into parallel fictional situations. If pencils are being stolen in your classroom, for example, you might develop a story about toys being stolen at a supervised playground.

You might also want to ask your students how different values conflict in their lives, saying something like "Have you ever wanted to keep a promise and tell the truth at the same time, but you couldn't do both? Tell me about the situation." Many children are very articulate about social dilemmas they face.

Keep your story as simple as possible, because children cannot handle a lot of variables simultaneously. Limit the number of characters, and do not introduce complications. Keep the language simple, of course, and the sentences relatively short.

Try to include characters of both sexes, especially if you plan role play rather than structured discussion. You want both boys and girls to have opportunities to play parts. Girls can take boys' parts and vice versa, but we find this often evokes jokes and silliness that distract from the goal (and are a management problem for you). One strategy that we find works fairly well is to present the story with its designated characters and then, during role play, change their sexes as necessary. You probably would not want to change the sex of the main characters, but supporting parts can be altered. This technique should be used only with older students; younger ones are too easily confused by departures from the story as originally presented.

Finally, after you have presented your story to the children, evaluate its effectiveness by asking yourself:

Did the children enjoy the story? Were they attentive?

Did they understand it? Did they give evidence of differentiating among characters? Did the children have any difficulties assuming roles?

Did any conflicts arise that you were not expecting? Was the story responsible for these conflicts? How?

What would you do differently next time? How would you do it?

6

The Roots of Decision Making

The Theories Behind It All

For twenty minutes, the structured discussion had been going well. The children had been unanimously concerned with the outcome of "Who Takes the Cake?" and, although it was only their second experience with structured discussion, they were having no trouble with its processes and concepts.

In "Who Takes the Cake?" the central character, Barbara, packs two pieces of cake for a picnic lunch because she plans to give one to her friend Ginny, who helped make the cake. There are two other children at the picnic, however, and one of them has forgotten his lunch. Barbara tries to decide what to do with the two pieces of cake, given the fact that Ginny has protested giving her own piece to the forgetful boy.

By now the class (a third grade) had made several suggestions. (1) Barbara could simply go with the original plan, and the boy would just have to get by on whatever tidbits other people shared with him. (2) The children could share everything they had brought, breaking every sandwich, apple, and other food item into four pieces. (3) The two pieces of cake could each be cut in half so that each of the four children could have the same amount. It was this last solution that caught the fancy of most of the children, and the majority eventually settled on it as the best solution. We prepared to move into the debriefing phase of the discussion.

Suddenly, in the middle of the room, a small hand began waving frantically. It belonged to Carla, one of the leaders in the class.

"Yes, Carla?"

"I think I have a better idea," she said, pausing and glancing around the room for effect. "I think that Barbara ought to split each piece of cake into four pieces. That way everybody could get two pieces of cake instead of just one."

A few children looked intensely interested. "Yeah," someone agreed, "that's a great idea!"

"Yeah," came a number of echoes.

We tried briefly to reason with the children. "You know," we said, "you still start out with the same amount of cake." The children all agreed on that. "So you won't end up with any more no matter how you cut it." The children had a harder time seeing that. A few did, but most agreed with Carla that more pieces meant more cake. When the debriefing drew to a close, the class had decided almost unanimously that splitting the cake into eight pieces ("so they'll have more") would be the best solution.

We had not predicted this turn of events. But we had studied theories of social development, and we knew we had just received practical confirmation of some theoretical lessons: (1) the development of social thinking is tied to cognitive development; (2) persuasive argument by a respected peer can affect the reasoning of an entire group of children; and (3) it is useless to try to argue children into a cognitive understanding of which they are not yet capable.

The basis for our analysis of this classroom experience is our acquaintance with the theoretical and practical work of Jean Piaget, Lawrence Kohlberg, William Damon, and Robert Selman (and, indirectly, Louis Raths and his coauthors; see our discussion of values clarification in the Introduction). These researchers have developed theories and practical ideas about social growth, as we mention in the Introduction. They influenced each other's thinking, and we, as authors of this book, have been influenced by all of them. You, as composers of decision stories and as educators using decision stories in classrooms, may find their reflections useful, too.

Piaget

Piaget is the earliest of the theorists we discuss. Observing children's responses to rules, laws, responsibility, and justice, Piaget concluded that social, or, more particularly, moral, development is linked to cognitive development. A child matures in moral thought *only* as he or she matures cognitively. Our Carla, for instance—and apparently most of her classmates—could not yet grasp that cutting a piece of cake does not increase its quantity. Her cognitive immaturity, coupled with her leadership qualities, temporarily affected the cognitive and moral thought of the class.

Piaget designates the first period of cognitive development, from birth to the age of eighteen months to two years, as the sensorimotor. During this period, children use motor activity and their physiological senses to solve problems, and it is through physical or sensory interaction with objects that they understand them. A toddler, for example, might learn not to touch a hot stove either because he has felt the consequences, or because his mother has scolded him in some way and said, sternly, "Hot!" Either way, the learning is sensorimotor, and the lesson applies only when the child is in the kitchen with the stove (and with his mother present, if her words were part of the lesson).

From the ages of roughly two to six, which Piaget calls the preoperational stage, the child learns to symbolize: to make one object or idea represent a different, absent one. Now if the child's mother is out of the kitchen, the child recalls the scolding and, one hopes, leaves the stove alone. Or he may see a picture of a stove in a magazine and say, "Hot!"

Generally, after the age of six, children become capable of concrete operations, and this capacity characterizes the next stage of cognitive development that Piaget describes. Now children are capable of real dialogue. The mother can explain that she is cooking, that the stove will be hot, and that the child should play in another room until she has finished. Although the child might be disappointed, he can understand her, possibly see her point of view, and agree to cooperate.

Piaget says the final period, that of formal operations, begins at age eleven or twelve and extends throughout adulthood. The child in this stage can think with increasing complexity and can handle abstract ideas; thought no longer has to be concretely based.

Piaget's exploration of moral development was brief compared to his extensive research into cognitive growth. He outlines three stages of moral growth but does not describe them complexly. He calls the three stages the heteronomous, in which the morality is one of constraint; the intermediate, a bridge between the first and third; and the autonomous, in which the morality is one of cooperation. The heteronomous stage lasts until the age of seven or eight; the intermediate, until eleven or twelve.

Heteronomy, which roughly coincides with the preoperational cognitive period, is characterized by a belief that good is essentially an obedience to given rules; whether or not they are just is irrelevant. Further, obedience to adult authority is rigidly interpreted, as is the letter, rather than the spirit, of the law. Finally, a child is likely to think someone should be punished according to the scope of his or her misdeed, rather than according to motivation. Our child at the stove is not likely to reason that there may be good and bad times to touch the burner. He is simply concerned with doing what his mother has said to do, thereby winning praise for being good, and, of course, avoiding a scolding.

In the intermediate stage, children begin to favor the principle of punishment befitting crime; autonomy and egalitarianism emerge, too. Motivation is now considered relevant to questions of justice. Cooperation and reciprocity are also considerations. (None of these principles is firmly established in the children's thought, however.) Now a neighborhood friend, according to our child in the kitchen, should be excused for touching the stove if she did not know better. Previously, he would have insisted she be punished for disobeying a rule, despite her ignorance of it.

The final stage is characterized by autonomy and cooperation. Movement from stage to stage depends on cognitive maturity, but home and school provide influences, too. Now, unless there is a long history of hearing "Don't touch it because I said so!" the child should be able to see all the physical consequences of stove touching, and social ramifications, as well: he will try to set a proper example for younger children, for instance, and be considerate of a busy mother by staying away from the hot stove at which she is cooking, so as not to add to her concerns.

Kohlberg

In the last twenty years or so, Lawrence Kohlberg has further researched and extended Piaget's theory of moral development. Basically, the two agree on the linkage between moral and cognitive development. Based on his original work with boys aged ten to sixteen, Kohlberg defines three developmental levels of moral judgment, each comprising two stages. Each second stage adds depth and sophistication to the first.

In level one, stage one, the child believes that submission to authority constitutes right action. The child values obedience in and of itself, sees right as simply whatever those in authority reward, and defines wrong as whatever brings punishment. At this stage, a child does not understand things from other people's points of view.

In level one, stage two, a child no longer blindly follows rules for their own sake; the child is willing to bend rules to serve his or her own interests. At the same time, the child understands that others also have interests, and that it is sometimes necessary to work reciprocal deals in order to be fair.

Kohlberg holds that most children younger than nine are at level one, as are some adolescents and criminal offenders.

Level two is the highest level achieved by most adults. It involves an understanding of responsibility to a group and commitment to upholding laws. Level three is reached by a minority of adults who come to value the principles underlying formulated laws, or who abide by universal ethical principles that may conflict at times with human laws (Kohlberg suggests Christ, Gandhi, and Martin Luther King, Jr., as examples of those abiding by such principles).

Unlike Piaget, who simply reports observations of moral development, Kohlberg advocates moral education as a means of encouraging people to expand their awareness of the higher moral stages and to aspire to them in their judgments. Kohlberg's ideas on teaching techniques have evolved over the years, but the techniques are based primarily on discussion of moral dilemmas, either hypothetical or experienced. Class discussion along these lines may be part of the social studies, history, or English curriculum. Moral development is not to be taught as a subject in itself, however; it should be a part of classroom life.

Damon

Although Kohlberg posits stages of moral development beginning in early childhood, he confines his research to children ten and older, and he relies on Piaget for an analysis of development in the early years. William Damon, however, has explored social reasoning in younger children extensively, and he has found that, by and large, Piaget's and Kohlberg's ideas of side-by-side cognitive and social development are sound. Damon's research, based on interviews with young children, offers a view in some depth of this co-development. One aspect of children's thought on which Damon has focused is the idea of fairness in sharing (sharing, he says, is probably the most important factor in children's friendships). Fairness— justice—in sharing is important to all children; but at different ages, children conceptualize this positive justice (as Damon terms it) differently.

At what Damon calls level 0-A, a child equates positive justice with, basically, selfish fulfillment; the child argues, "I should get it because I want it."

At level 0-B, the child still equates positive justice with receiving what he or she wants but now tries to justify his or her claims by appeals to external facts, offering such arguments as "We should get the most because we're girls."

At level 1-A, children equate positive justice with strict equality. ("Everyone should get the same, no matter what.")

At level 1-B, children base their notion of positive justice on ideas of reciprocity, merit, and deservingness. ("He did something nice for me, so I should do something nice for him." "She did the most work; she should get the most.")

At level 2-A, children grasp the notion of moral relativity—the idea that different people may justify their claims differently. Children also begin to believe that people in special circumstances (the poor, for example) should receive special consideration. Children attempt quantitative compromises ("He should get the most, but she should get some, too").

At level 2-B, children coordinate considerations of equality and reciprocity. Various claims are considered, as well as the peculiar demands of each situation. At this stage, children believe that all involved should receive their due, although this may not mean mathematically even distribution. ("This kid with none should get more than the other kid who already has some, even if they both did the same amount of work.")

Damon indicates that four-year-olds are normally at level 0-A or 0-B; five-year-olds and some older children, at 1-A; six- and seven-year-olds, at 1-B; and eight- to ten-year-olds, at 2-A or 2-B.

Recall the structured discussion about Barbara's two pieces of cake. During the twenty minutes that these third graders discussed what should be done about this sharing dilemma, they consistently returned to the problem of the boy who had forgotten his lunch (while not neglecting the prior claim of Ginny, who had helped make the cake). Thus, their reasoning was generally at level 2-A or 2-B. (Yet, when it came time to make the hard choice, some were sidetracked by their poorly developed cognitive skills.)

Because he is a psychologist and not a teacher, Damon has had more interest in observing children than in education for social growth. But in the research we did, using role play and structured discussion with third graders and children in other grades, we found it possible to help children advance in their notions of positive justice.

Selman

Robert Selman is, like Damon, a psychologist interested in children's social development. He, too, has been strongly influenced by Piaget and Kohlberg and has focused his research on one area of their theory and its influence on the judgment of children. This area is termed social perspective taking, which amounts basically to imagining oneself in someone else's shoes, understanding how that person thinks and feels about a situation. Selman, like Piaget, Kohlberg, and Damon, has interviewed children to explore their abilities at various ages and has determined that children do, indeed, pass through recognizable stages of growth in ability to see things from others' points of view.

At stage zero, according to Selman, three- to six-year-olds are egocentric, failing to distinguish between the social perspectives of themselves and others. They can recognize others' overt expressions of feeling, however. ("Mommy's crying, so I'll give her my teddy bear.")

In stage one, six- to eight-year-olds are aware that others have their own perspectives that may differ from the children's own, but children at this stage tend to focus on one viewpoint without being able to coordinate different feelings. ("If I take the cookie, my sister will be unhappy; but I want it, so I'll take it.")

In stage two, eight- to ten-year-olds acknowledge conflicting feelings about social situations, but the children do not experience these feelings as really mixed. Instead, they feel them one at a time or as if in different parts of the mind. ("If I did that, first I'd be happy, and then I'd be sad.")

In stage three, ten- to twelve-year-olds can step outside a social situation and view it from a third-person standpoint. They now understand that people can have really mixed reactions to situations or even be unaware of their own true feelings.

Selman has not confined himself to observation and description. He has introduced discussion into elementary classrooms to see if children become more capable of taking others' perspectives as a result. Recognizing the need to make these discussions concrete, he has relied on a series of filmstrips, and he has indeed been successful in improving children's perspective-taking skills. In our research, we have found that concrete strategies (role play and structured discussion) help children grow in ability to put themselves in other people's shoes.

The Developmental Viewpoint

Piaget, Kohlberg, Damon, and Selman have studied children at various stages of social and cognitive development. Although each of the four has his preferred formulation, all four agree on some fundamental conclusions.

First of all, cognitive and social growth are interrelated. Further, cognitive maturity is necessary for social or moral maturity, but the reverse is not true; a child can develop cognitively without growing in corresponding social understanding. These researchers also agree that children progress through the various developmental stages in consecutive order; a child cannot skip a stage. Finally, they all believe that social interaction influences—in fact, determines—a child's social development.

The following chart shows the similarities among the stages each researcher defines, however different the terminology.

Stages of Cognitive and Moral Development, Ages Two Through Eleven (all ages approximate)

AGE	PIAGET (cognitive)	PIAGET (moral)
2		**Heteronomous Morality** Moral absolutism Belief in immutability of rules Belief in inevitability of punishment for wrongdoing Judgment of act by its consequences Equating wrongness with what is forbidden Belief in arbitrary punishment Approval of authority-based punishment of peers Approval of arbitrary distribution of resources Belief that duty is obedience to authority
3	**Preoperational Cognition** Emergence of thought Internal representation of objects Development of language Cognitive egocentrism Difficulty distinguishing reality from fantasy Prelogical thought	
4		
5		
6		
		Transition
7	**Concrete Operational Cognition** Reversible mental actions Thought generally in terms of concrete objects Few abstractions Ability to classify Ability to conserve	**Autonomous Morality** Awareness of differing viewpoints View of rules as flexible Naturalistic conception of punishment Willingness to consider agent's intentions in judging an act Equating of wrongness with what violates spirit of cooperation Belief in restitution or reciprocity in punishment Approval of equal retaliation by victim Approval of equal distribution Belief that duty is allegiance to equality or common welfare
8		
9		
10		
11		

KOHLBERG (moral)	DAMON (positive justice)	SELMAN (perspective taking)
	Level 0-A Basing of choices on egocentric wishes	
	Level 0-B Basing of choices on own desires, with external justification offered	
Preconventional Morality **Stage 1 – Heteronomy** Egocentric point of view Avoidance of punishment Belief in superior power of authorities Avoidance of physical damage to persons, property **Stage 2 – Individualism** Following of rules when in own interest Belief that right is what's fair, equal exchange, a deal Awareness that others have their own interests, too	**Level 1-A** Commitment to strict equality when making choices	**Stage 0 – Egocentric Role Taking** Differentiation of self and other as entities, but not in terms of their points of view
	Level 1-B Commitment to reciprocity when making choices	**Stage 1 – Social-Informational Role Taking** Realization that people think and feel differently in different situations or with different information Recognition of difference between intentional and unintentional actions by self and others
	Level 2-A Moral relativity: belief that different persons can have equally valid justifications for choices	
Conventional Morality **Stage 3 – Mutuality, Conformity** Belief that being good is important Belief in Golden Rule Commitment to living up to expectations	**Level 2-B** Consideration of various claims and situational demands when making choices	**Stage 2 – Self-Reflective Role Taking** Relativistic belief that no person's perspective is absolutely right Ability to view own behavior and motivation from outside self

Further Reading

Many psychologists and educators agree that teachers can help children grow in moral understanding and behavior. Research results are quite positive in this regard. You might enjoy reading about that research, and related theories, both for their own sake, and because, as we have said, they underlie our recommendations in this book.

Chesler, Mark, and Robert Fox. 1966. *Role-Playing Methods in the Class-room*. Chicago: Science Research Associates.

A concise description of role-playing methods and strategies is followed by approximately 100 problems that can be role-played. The book is similar to Shaftel and Shaftel's.

Damon, William. 1977. *The Social World of the Child.* San Francisco: Jossey-Bass.

A broad range of social issues in the lives of young children has been studied by the author, a developmental psychologist. He sees in children much the same development as Piaget describes, but Damon explores it in more detail and depth. The author discusses his research and the developmental levels he discovers in children's social reasoning.

Fraenkel, Jack R. 1977. *How To Teach About Values: An Analytic Approach.* Englewood Cliffs, N.J.: Prentice-Hall.

Although Fraenkel's suggestions are for teachers of older students, his critical discussions of Piaget, Kohlberg, and the values clarification approach are instructive and useful to teachers at any level. The book contains a good discussion of the philosophy of values in relation to the school experience.

Galbraith, Ronald E., and Thomas M. Jones. 1976. *Moral Reasoning: A Teaching Handbook for Adapting Kohlberg to the Classroom.* Anoka, Minn.: Greenhaven Press.

The book offers practical strategies for employing the moral-reasoning approach in classrooms; the underlying theory of moral development is Kohlberg's. Although the book is directed to teachers of older students, one chapter is devoted to adapting the moral-reasoning approach to elementary grades. Three moral dilemmas appropriate to younger children are presented.

Hersh, Richard, Diana Paolitto, and Joseph Reimer. 1979. *Promoting Moral Growth.* New York: Longman.

For teachers of middle and higher grades, this book suggests teaching strategies based on Piaget's and Kohlberg's theories of moral development. The first half of the book is useful for teachers of younger children; it explains the theories of Piaget and Kohlberg with great clarity.

Lickona, Thomas, ed. 1976. *Moral Development and Behavior.* New York: Holt, Rinehart and Winston.

This collection of writings by theorists and researchers presents various views of moral and value development, including some we do not discuss in the present volume. Of special interest is Robert Selman's chapter on social perspective taking.

Mussen, Paul, and Nancy Eisenberg-Berg. 1977. *Roots of Caring, Sharing and Helping.* San Francisco: W.H. Freeman.

The authors offer an excellent overview of moral development research to 1977 and suggest further research.

Piaget, Jean. 1932 [original publication date]. *The Moral Judgment of the Child.* New York: The Free Press, 1965.

This classic represents Piaget's relatively brief research into children's moral development. The book contains Piaget's argument that moral and cognitive development are not only related but interdependent, his description of three major stages of moral development, and numerous observations of and quotations from children.

Raths, Louis E., Merrill Harmin, and Sidney B. Simon. 1978. *Values and Teaching.* Columbus, Ohio: Charles E. Merrill.

This is the principal handbook on values clarification as a teaching technique. It is geared to teachers of students in junior or senior high school. The background discussion may interest teachers of young children, however, and a few of the teaching techniques could perhaps be adapted to the early grades.

Selman, Robert L. 1980. *The Growth of Interpersonal Understanding.* New York: Academic Press.

Within Piaget and Kohlberg's theoretical framework, Selman has devoted his considerable research to one aspect of moral development: social perspective taking, the ability to see someone else's point of view that is a precondition for moral growth. The book offers an explanation of Selman's research and the theory behind it; it is helpful to other researchers and those interested in exploring moral development theory in depth.

Shaftel, Fannie, and George Shaftel. 1982. *Role Playing in the Curriculum.* 2nd ed. Englewood Cliffs, N.J.: Prentice-Hall.

The first part of this book explains role play in depth: the process itself, teaching techniques it involves, and reasons for using it in elementary classrooms. The last half of the book describes the use of open-ended stories (dealing with such topics as honesty, responsibility, friendship, and self-acceptance) that are suitable for use with role play in all areas of the elementary curriculum.

Simon, Sidney B., Leland W. Howe, and Howard Kirschenbaum. 1978. *Values Clarification: A Handbook of Practical Strategies for Teachers and Students.* New York: Hart.

As its title implies, this book is devoted to specific activities promoting the clarification of students' values. Some of the seventy-nine exercises can be used with, or adapted to, younger children. An introductory section describes the process of values clarification.